REVOLUTION DETROIT

REVOLUTION DETROIT

Strategies for Urban Reinvention

John Gallagher

Detroit, Michigan

17 16 15 14 13   5 4 3 2 1

Library of Congress Cataloging-in-Publication Data

Gallagher, John, 1949–

Revolution Detroit : strategies for urban reinvention / John Gallagher.
p. cm.
Includes bibliographical references and index.
ISBN 978-0-8143-3871-1 (pbk. : alk. paper) — ISBN 978-0-8143-3857-5 (ebook)
1. Urban renewal—Michigan—Detroit. 2. Detroit (Mich.)—Politics and government—
21st century. 3. Detroit (Mich.)—Social conditions—21st century. 4. Detroit (Mich.)—
Economic conditions—21st century. I. Title.
HT177.D4G353 2013
307.3'4160977434—dc23
2012030202

This book has been printed on 100 percent postconsumer recycled paper made
from wood grown in FSC-certified forests.

Designed by Brad Norr Design
Typeset by Maya Rhodes
Composed in Bell Centennial and Serifa

Parts of chapter 1, "Detroit Today," appeared in somewhat different form in the author's
introductory essay to the Detroit Revealed photography catalog produced by the Detroit
Institute of Arts.

To my wife, Sheu-Jane, and to my parents, Helen and John

Sweet are the uses of adversity.

—As You Like It

CONTENTS

It's a truism that one question always leads to another. Certainly my own perspective on our distressed cities grew exponentially after Wayne State University Press published my previous book, *Reimagining Detroit: Opportunities for Redefining an American City*, in late 2010. Four events stemmed from that book's publication that immeasurably added to the content and dimension of this new one.

First, the publication of *Reimagining Detroit* led to invitations to speak to many people in many venues, from universities in and around Detroit to urban planning conferences in Europe. The audiences ranged from no more than eight people at one suburban Detroit library to twelve hundred people at the annual Book & Author Society lunch in Detroit. The questions asked by the audiences honed my understanding of my own material—material I had assumed (incorrectly) that I had already mastered; their questions sent me off in search of new facts and new insights on cities. Next, *Reimagining Detroit* also led to an invitation from the German Marshall Fund of the United States to accompany a tour of European post-industrial cities—specifically Leipzig, Germany, and Manchester, England—in late 2010. This tour, which included colleagues from Detroit, Flint, Cleveland, Youngstown, and Pittsburgh, packed enough interviews and insights into a short span to fill my reporter's notebooks and give me a list of contacts that has led to many fruitful conversations. Third, the earlier book garnered an invitation from the American Assembly, a roving think tank founded by Dwight D. Eisenhower that considers a host of important issues facing America, to attend the assembly's four-day conference on remaking distressed urban cities, held in Detroit in 2011. That intense experience likewise produced numerous helpful insights into the urban dilemma of today. Finally, a friend and Detroit-based filmmaker, Carrie LeZotte of One of Us Films, decided to make a documentary inspired by *Reimagining Detroit*, with me serving as co-producer and writer as we filmed in Detroit, Philadelphia, Youngstown, and other cites. The many hours of conversations with people in all those cities during the shooting, plus the site visits in each city, gave me much new material. All of these results—the give-and-take of speaking engagements, my visits to Leipzig and Manchester, the fruit of the American Assembly discussions, the interviews for the documentary film—led directly to this new book.

As a journalist, I'm often surprised when some people call me an optimist about Detroit's chances. Having visited all parts of my deeply troubled city, having talked to its people, and having chronicled its many failures and its occasional successes, I prefer to think of myself as a sober realist about the city. But realism need not mean despair. Detroit as well as Flint and Manchester and Leipzig and Cleveland and Youngstown and many other post-industrial cities do show successes as well as failures, successes that stem from innovative ways of thinking and acting. Moreover, these successes are far from trivial. In city after city, we can point to new ways of governing, new ways of repurposing old industrial sites, new entrepreneurial models to replace the older, often vanished economy, and new approaches to schools and crime and vacant urban places. This book visits many of those cities and tries to draw some reasonable lessons from their example. If something works in one city, it's worth trying elsewhere. If that makes me an optimist, then I guess I plead guilty.

Visiting the National Gallery of Art in Washington, D.C., not long ago, I stopped before *Boulevard des Italiens*, Camille Pissarro's lustrous depiction of Paris in the 1890s. "Now *that's* a city," I said to myself. Pissarro painted it not long after Baron von Haussmann muscled his grand vision for Paris through the twisty byways of the medieval town. Subtitled *Morning Sunlight*, the painting depicts one of the broad boulevards that von Haussmann created, filled with carriages and people and elegant buildings. Pissarro suffused his Paris not just with the glow of morning, but with the essence of urban vitality—that dense brew of talent and art and commerce that, the world over, has produced human triumphs as varied as the Renaissance, democracy, the four-star restaurant, and the public library.

Now consider a second portrait of a city, this one a photograph I took of Detroit's far-east side on a summer morning in 2010. A field of tall grass and Queen Anne's lace rises gently to the horizon; a split-rail fence traverses the foreground; there are no people, no roads, no vehicles, no buildings—nothing to trigger the words "urban" and "cities" in our brains. A city-owned site where local fishermen dangle lines into the nearby Detroit River, it represents one of the numerous voids in Detroit's urban landscape. Within a few blocks I can find a half-dozen more sites as large and as vacant; within a mile, dozens more. These are places where open fields run block after block, where the houses and factories have vanished, and from where the residents fled long ago. Yet this, too, is a city, albeit a troubled one; even in today's emptied-out state, Detroit at the 2010 Census remained a city of more than seven hundred thousand people, a city whose population equaled that of Cleveland and Pittsburgh combined; a city where roughly twice as many people squeeze in per square mile than in places like Dallas and Houston and Phoenix, which are so spread out over so many

Camille Pissarro's depiction of Paris in the 1890s captures the essence of urban vitality. (Courtesy of the National Gallery of Art)

hundreds of square miles that each resembles more of a giant suburb than a city like Paris in the 1890s or New York or Mumbai today.

Detroit once resembled *Boulevard des Italiens.* As recently as the 1950s, a photograph of downtown Detroit overlaid on Pissarro's painting would fit almost exactly, the only difference being the vehicles were Fords and Chevys and not horse-drawn carriages. But since the mid-twentieth-century heyday of industrial cities, Detroit, Cleveland, St. Louis, Buffalo, Flint, and so many more have lost people and jobs and industry, sliding down a path that takes them from *Boulevard des Italiens* toward something more like where Detroit finds itself today, if not to the same degree, at least in kind. If many of the world's urban places grow at an uncontrollable pace—megalopolises like Mumbai and Sao Paulo and Shanghai, and, to a lesser degree, places like Phoenix and Los

Angeles—many other urban centers the world over are heading in the direction of where Detroit finds itself today, a city so drained of its lifeblood that it can no longer govern itself in the traditional way, can no longer provide jobs for large numbers of its people, and can no longer find productive uses for great swaths of urban landscape slowly returning to nature.

Bridging the gap between the urbanism of *Boulevard des Italiens* and the voids we see in Detroit provides the theme of this book. To put it another way, how do we reinvent the once great but now humbled cities of which Detroit is merely the most represented example? There are almost too many of these thinned-out cities to count; certainly the number worldwide stands in the hundreds.

"This is an international phenomenon," my friend Robin Boyle, the chair of the Department of Urban Planning at Wayne State University in Detroit, told me during one of our many conversations. "Even in areas in Asia, we are seeing the change occurring. Parts of Japan, for example, have got areas where the old manufacturing activities have moved elsewhere, leaving a smaller, older set of communities that are struggling with the process of urban change."

We'll tour many of these distressed cities in this book, making stops in Cleveland and Philadelphia and others in this country, and Manchester, England,

Planners estimate that up to forty square miles of Detroit's 139-square-mile footprint now consists of vacant lots, unkempt parks, abandoned public rights-of-way, and other vacancy. (Author photo)

and Leipzig, Germany, abroad. All these post-industrial cities have been struggling to reinvent themselves, their economies, their governing models, their urban fabric.

What to call these places lately has provoked considerable debate. German thinkers came up with the term "shrinking cities" a while ago, and that term has caught on, although not everyone likes it. For one thing, many of these cities, including Detroit, aren't really shrinking at all if we look at their broader metropolitan areas. Metro Detroit's population today is fifty percent bigger than it was in 1950, and much the same could be said of other "shrinking" cities like Cleveland and Philadelphia. Indeed, if you look at America's fifty largest cities in 1950, twenty-six have lost population since then, but *all* have gained residents in their broader metropolitan regions, the suburbs gaining at the expense of the older city. Our great industrial centers did not shrink so much as they spread out following World War II, plowing up nearby farmland to create a new low-density landscape ruled by the private automobile.

Disliking the negative tone of "shrinking," the American Assembly, a roving think tank based at Columbia University in New York, met for four days in Detroit in 2011 to discuss urban reinvention and, on a whim, offered the dozens of assembled planners, government officials, academics, and handful of media reporters like me a prize of one hundred dollars to come up with a more appropriate term. The winner was "legacy cities," the notion being that these cities carry a heritage of prestige and power, the remnants of which command respect even today. A good number of people objected that "legacy" carries negative tones in a post-industrial city; legacy costs are those that a company finds a burden and tries to shed. But the assembly adopted the term over the objections, and "legacy cities" has attained a modest currency. In this book I will use several terms to refer to cities like Detroit, including both legacy and shrinking, on the theory that what we call them is less important than understanding them. Personally I don't believe we need any adjective before "city" to describe these places, because any such usage implies these places are different from "thriving" cities like the Sunbelt capitals and megalopolises like Shanghai and Mumbai. They're not. They're all cities, just in different spots in the cycle of growth and decline and rebirth.

The word "city" can refer to many different things—a town's population, its culture, its economy, its geographic features, its sports teams, its "brand," and so on—and the outlook for each can be fortunate or troubled. But the weakest link in city after city is the municipal corporation, the city government. City governments today, in Detroit and elsewhere, teeter on the brink of bankruptcy or at least financial danger, their departments underfunded, understaffed, and hobbled by political dysfunction. The failure of city governments began in the years after World War II, when jobs and people began to leave for the suburbs, taking their cities' tax base with them. For a brief while, everyone thought it a healthy trend, relieving some of the congestion in the inner city. And certainly automotive companies and road builders and real-estate developers eagerly anticipated the push into the cornfields, because urban sprawl would guarantee decades of work and profits for them. Soon, though—certainly by around 1960— leaders in the older central cities realized they had a problem on their hands. Detroit, for example, lost close to ten percent of its population in the 1950s and almost ten percent more in the '60s, and then, in the 1970s—after the 1967 riots that wracked Detroit—just over twenty percent of the city's population left. They left behind a landscape of slowly emptying factories and stores and houses, a landscape that neither bright slogan nor clever tax credit would ever fill up again.

There is a rich literature on the subject of urban decline, and scholars and historians have pinned the blame on a complex mix of federal subsidies for homebuilders in the suburbs, the expanding network of expressways, redlining by bankers and insurance companies, and much more. All of these played a role, along with the poisonous race conflicts in places like Detroit that sent the white middle class heading for the exits. But in this vast literature of urban decline, perhaps we don't pay enough attention to the desirability of the suburban lifestyle as a draw.

Consider the attached garage. This innovation—allowing suburban homemakers to carry their groceries inside the house without exposure to the rain and snow—began to appear as a feature of newly built houses around 1960 or so, first as a single-car garage, then a two-car garage, and in today's McMansions it comes in three- or four-car varieties. But this innovation came along just as many traditional cities like Detroit had already built out to their borders and were pushing into the farmland nearby. It meant that homebuyers looking for the popular new style had to go outside the city to find it. The same is true of central air conditioning and other post–World War II advances in home design. Homes were getting bigger, too; many working-class cottages in Detroit measured less than a thousand square feet; by 1974 the median size of a newly built house in America grew to 1,560 square feet, and by 2011 the median size of a new house had swelled to 2,235 square feet. Older neighborhoods in the central cities could boast of their distinguished architecture, their hardwood floors and leaded glass windows, but that represented an older form of luxury; the new form, which buyers by the millions were seeking, involved bigger kitchens and newer appliances and central air and attached garages. All these innovations drew homebuyers out of the city.

That this new lifestyle was so different from the old became immediately obvious to anyone who made the transition. In about 1970, Peter Karmanos Jr., a rising software entrepreneur, Detroit native, and city resident with a young family, started shopping for a home in the suburbs. He and his family bought one in a growing community called West Bloomfield, "taking every cent I had," Karmanos told me many years later. The Labor Day weekend they moved in, Karmanos took a beer out to his deck. The afternoon air was alive with the sound of power lawnmowers. Back in the city, where home lawns were postage-stamp sized, no one had ever needed a power mower. Karmanos said to himself, "I think this is a little different from where I came from."

Generations of urban affairs writers have mocked the suburbs as a cultural wasteland, but for two or three generations of families, the suburbs provided a place with big homes and yards, decent schools, safety, and easy access along a growing network of expressways and major roads to seemingly all that one needed. In this sense, all those families who migrated out of Flint and Gary and Rochester and St. Louis weren't fleeing distress so much as following the dream of a new lifestyle. Racial animosity often made the process an ugly one, and racial and economic injustice accelerated the flight from the city. Yet we err if we don't realize that it was also the promise ahead, not just the problems behind, that drew people on; the black middle class left places like Detroit as quickly as the white middle class once they had the means.

The same is true, of course, of industry, which began pushing out of Detroit and other cities as early as the 1940s to find more room. Detroit in the first two or three decades of the twentieth century created some of the most innovative factories in the world, but by the 1950s, those early factories had grown out of date. Indeed, any big auto plant operating in Detroit today has been completely rebuilt, often by razing an early twentieth-century version and starting over. The Detroit model of a city, built to its zenith in the years between 1900 and 1960, simply couldn't offer the same capacity and amenities as newer model urban places just beyond the city's borders.

Older cities in Europe were going through much the same process; about forty percent of the largest cities in Europe have lost population during the past few decades. Reasons vary. Turin, Italy, much like Detroit, lost its automotive industry. Manchester, England, saw its cotton mills and other industry disappear. Leipzig, Germany, saw many residents flee to the former West Germany after German reunification in 1990. Everything from low birth rates to political upheaval can cause a city to shrink.

If the older industrial cities in the United States tumbled in the population rankings, newer Sunbelt cities took their place—Los Angeles, Houston, Phoenix, Dallas, and the like. But cities that showed Brobdingnagian growth did so largely through a sort of legal and demographic sleight of hand. *They annexed their suburbs as they grew.* After World War II, annexation was denied to Detroit, Cleveland, Pittsburgh, and other older Midwest and Northeast cities, trapped behind their ossified municipal boundaries by legal or constitutional restrictions. Not so in the Sunbelt. Dallas covered 112 square miles in 1950; today it sprawls out over 340 square miles. San Antonio's land area grew by more than six hundred percent, from sixty-nine square miles in 1950 to 460 today. Houston started out in 1950 covering roughly the same square mileage as Detroit— Houston with 160 square miles and Detroit with 139; today Houston stretches out over six hundred square miles. The City of Phoenix covers roughly ten times as much land area today as it did in the late 1950s.

Annexation isn't the only reason those cities grew, of course; buoyant economies and endless sunshine in the South and Southwest drew millions of newcomers. But one must ask: What if Detroit had been permitted to annex suburbs after World War II? What if it had grown to, say, the square mileage of Houston today? If so, Detroit's population would hover today somewhere around three million people, ranking it the nation's third largest city, behind only New York and Los Angeles.

Just for a moment, think about what a difference it would have made in Detroit's story if the city had been allowed to adjust its borders as Sunbelt cities could. Instead of a city today defined as among the poorest in the nation, it would show an admirable diversity of incomes. Its population, today more than eighty percent African American, would offer much greater racial and ethnic complexity. The failures of the school system and city policing might have been leavened by the inclusion of more middle-class areas. A tax base that was growing, not shrinking, could have provided the cash needed to deal more efficiently with incipient blight and economic challenges.

We cannot, of course, undo history. But we cannot miss how a lack of regional reach led to—and in fact defines—the plight of these older industrial cities.

By the 1970s, the shrinking city had become a disgrace in America, and civic leaders tried heroic measures to reverse the trends. Federal aid for cities poured in, contractors built model neighborhoods, and big showcase projects like Detroit's Renaissance Center went up (ironically adding to the problem by creating a fortress on the riverfront all but totally shut off from the rest of the city). City planners threw multiple tax breaks for rebuilding into the breach. Yet the drain continued. As of the 2010 census, the old central city of Detroit contained just seventeen percent of its metropolitan population, about average for one of our shrinking cities. Cleveland contains nineteen percent of its metrowide population, Buffalo twenty-three percent, Baltimore twenty-two percent, Cincinnati fourteen percent, and St. Louis a mere eleven percent.

Jobs provide an even surer clue to the fiscal distress of today's central cities. Back in 1972, the US Census Bureau's survey of manufacturers found 2,398 manufacturing facilities in the city of Detroit employing 180,000 workers, or about twelve percent of the city's population. By 2007, the survey found just 472 facilities employing 22,962 workers, or only about three percent of the city's residents.

But the tax base, the total value of real estate in a community on which owners pay property taxes to support local governments, provides the bleakest clue. Detroit today holds just six percent of the combined city-suburban tax base; Cleveland twelve percent of its regional tax base; St. Louis 8.9 percent; and the Philadelphia-Trenton, NJ, core cities about eleven percent of their regional tax base. The conclusion is inescapable: in many ways, the suburbs have become the city, reversing the historical role of the central urban core.

And it's not just that much of the tax base has moved out to the suburbs; equally distressing is that much of what's left behind in the older city doesn't pay taxes at all. The "Eds and Meds"—universities and hospitals providing much of the employment remaining in cities today—operate as nonprofit institutions exempt from local property taxes. Wayne State University, employing more than six thousand people, ranks as one of Detroit's biggest employers, with more staffers on its payroll in the city itself than either General Motors or Chrysler. WSU's campus occupies a prized chunk of the city's Midtown district. But Wayne State, as a nonprofit educational institution, pays no property taxes, nor do most of the other largest employers in the city, including the Detroit Public Schools and the Henry Ford Health System, although they of course do contribute in other ways, providing thousands of well-paying jobs.

When I worked as a young reporter in Rochester, NY, in the late 1970s, the Eastman Kodak Company employed more than sixty thousand workers in the city and pumped millions of dollars a year into the city's property-tax coffers; as I write this now in early 2012, Kodak employs fewer than seven thousand workers in Rochester and, having declared bankruptcy, will probably employ even fewer to come, while the University of Rochester and its related hospitals, the city's biggest employers, pay no property taxes. In Detroit, only about forty percent of the parcels in the city produce any tax revenue, once we remove all the nonprofit institutions like the universities, churches, and medical facilities, all publicly owned properties like parks and schools, and all the vacant buildings and open land on which nobody pays taxes anymore.

Boston is not only home to multiple universities but serves as its state's capital, filling the city with a rich variety of educational institutions and government buildings, not to mention museums and hospitals. But all these nonprofit institutions leave more than half of the city's land exempt from property taxes. Boston mayor Thomas Menino has been nudging the city's nonprofits to make greater voluntary payments in lieu of taxes, but with mixed results so far. In other cities, suggestions that the Eds and Meds pay fixed fees in lieu of taxes have met stiff resistance.

Sheila Cockrel, a longtime member of the Detroit City Council who now teaches government at Wayne State University, suggested in a conversation with me that the entire property tax system—upon which municipal government in America rests—needs reform or replacement. The globalization of banking and debt means that people are making decisions in far parts of the globe that may raise or lower the interest rate a Detroiter pays on a mortgage, thus indirectly affecting the value of one's home. And, Cockrel notes, as long as that's happening, property taxes—based on home values—become and remain very volatile. "And you cannot provide services based on volatility," Cockrel told me. "If the volatility is within a certain spread you can live with it, but not when it's become as completely volatile as it is now. That's devastating to this city's— any city's—ability to provide service, because property taxes don't pay for it."

By 2012, the legacy of long-term drain to the suburbs plus the bludgeoning of the Great Recession left many cities close to insolvency. Public officials, media commentators, business leaders, and the like often suggest steps that amount to short-term balance-sheet fixes. These include laying off municipal workers, cutting back on their overtime pay, trimming their health benefits and pension payments, canceling or delaying capital projects, and more of the same. These steps may help short-term cash flow, but they do nothing to solve the essential long-term problem facing cities. The problem is not that cops make too much overtime, or that politicians waste tax revenue or corruptly skim dollars off the top, or even that the Great Recession and the collapse of the national housing market has put cities into a unique bind. All these factors may contribute, of course. But they fail to get at the heart of the problem—the draining of jobs, population, and the tax base to the suburbs over several decades.

"The problem is not one of short-term fiscal stress at times of national economic crisis," write Alan Mallach and Eric Scorsone of the Center for Community Progress in a recent paper. "Nor is it principally a problem of poor management or inefficient service delivery, although both may be present. *The central problem is a structural one, built into the dynamics of the American city.*" As long as such huge imbalances exist between city and suburban tax bases, as long as state governments (which make the laws that create and govern cities) ignore the regional nature of municipal problems and potential solutions, we cannot solve the problem of municipal finance.

Nor will yet another round of cost cutting do any more than get strapped city treasuries through another fiscal year or two. Bettie Buss, an analyst with the respected Citizens Research Council of Michigan, has studied Detroit's budget problems for years. "You can't cut your way out of this," Buss told me in 2011. Detroit employed just shy of thirty thousand municipal workers in 1970; by 2011, it had cut its workforce to eleven thousand. It levies the highest property tax rates in the state, the highest city income tax rate; it charges a utility tax that few residents realize they pay; the city pockets tens of millions of dollars in casino dollars each year from Detroit's three gaming enterprises; and it has borrowed millions of dollars to pay its bills. All this, yet Detroit remains mired in an unending fiscal swamp, and faces, as I write this in early 2012, an almost certain radical reordering under state-mandated financial review.

Detroit is not alone. Adjusted for inflation, the city of Saginaw, Michigan, collected, in 2008, only thirty percent of the tax revenues it did in the late 1970s. Flint, Michigan, cut its firefighting force from 252 to 118, or over fifty percent, between 2000 and 2011. Dayton, Ohio, reduced its municipal workforce during the same years by nearly thirty percent.

Such draconian cuts may appear necessary, especially to emergency managers installed by state fiat. But nip-and-tuck solutions fail to get at the primary structural problem. "In the absence of fundamental change, even if these cities can adopt balanced budgets, they are balanced only at the price of grossly inadequate public services, deferred maintenance and replacement of infrastructure and capital stock, and disproportionately high local taxes," write Mallach and Scorsone. "Short-term 'solutions' may end up making a city's long-term prospects even more problematic."

Healthier cities and suburban governments may face belt-tightening, too, but they start from a much better place than the older core city. In Birmingham, Michigan, an upscale suburb located several miles north of Detroit, the per-capita tax base measures more than eight times that of the city of Detroit.

And so we come to a basic conclusion. We cannot pick up somewhere close to ninety percent of a city's jobs, population, and tax base, move it to the suburbs, and expect what's left behind to function normally. It doesn't work anymore. It cannot work. Blaming teachers and municipal unions is a sideshow. The model broke a long time ago, and cannot be fixed without completely redesigning the system. There simply isn't enough tax base left for cities to draw on to provide a normal range of municipal services.

I stress this fact upfront because it motivates this entire book. The municipal model in America is broken, beyond repair, and it's time we stopped trying to patch and cobble, and time to get down to some basic reinvention. As long ago as 1940, an urban planner named Harland Bartholomew warned in a prophetic essay that American cities were in danger of "decentralization," an early term for sprawl. Bartholomew said it meant the disintegration of cities. Unless you come to Detroit, you may never realize how completely right he was.

Why care? Simple. There's no vision of America that works without these legacy cities reinventing themselves. By various estimates some forty-five million Americans live within the metro areas of these cities; these places even now contain a good portion of the nation's industrial might and technical know-how, not to mention some of the world's great museums, symphonies, universities, hospitals, and other cultural and financial institutions. These legacy cities dominate entire sections of the United States—the Northeast, Great Lakes, and Middle West. The problems vexing Americans today, from income inequality and class conflicts to inadequate education, health care, and public safety, fester most acutely in these cities.

Many believe, or fear, that once fallen from their peak of population and power, there's no end for these legacy cities but dissolution and disaster. Yet many of these distressed cities around the world have notched successes of reinvention. This record remains modest, but the successes are worth noting, and learning from, and even celebrating. Not even the most ardent fans of, say, Cleveland or Leipzig would deny that generations of work lie ahead. But we've been at the game of urban reinvention long enough now to say with modest certainty that some things work and some things don't; and in this book we'll examine that record and draw some conclusions.

I once interviewed a corporate manager whose company was going through a bad patch. When I asked him how he found the energy to come to work every day, he said in a matter-of-fact voice that, for a manager, dealing with challenges was his everyday lot, the very definition of his job, something he had trained for his entire career. Reinvention was an iterative process, he told me; you tried one thing, kept what worked, tried a variation, and kept at it. Those of us who work on cities can benefit, I think, from his phlegmatic attitude. As the current slogan has it (borrowed from wartime England), we need to "Keep Calm and Carry On."

In the chapters that follow, this book will look at important examples of reinvention drawn from the recent history of Detroit and many other cities, including Cleveland, Flint, Richmond, Philadelphia, and Youngstown, as well as overseas examples including Manchester and Leipzig. All these places have worked diligently on reinvention; as a planner in Manchester told me during my visit to England in late 2010, "We've been sweating a model of civic entrepreneurship bloody hard for twenty years."

With so much good experimental work behind us, we now have enough of a track record of urban reinvention to point to some best practices and to highlight the obvious errors. Detroit in particular can offer stories of both success and failure—and we can learn from both. But we'll be looking at many other places, too.

Before we begin, though, we must first take a closer look at Detroit as it stands today. Understanding this city in greater detail lays the groundwork for all that follows.

1

DETROIT TODAY

Real-estate developers in the upscale suburbs north of Detroit sometimes tell a joke when the conversation turns to rebuilding the Motor City. "We *did* rebuild the city of Detroit," they say. "We did it in Oakland County." That quip contains the key to understanding Detroit today—arguably America's most distressed big city. As early as the 1940s, auto companies were scouting for undeveloped land outside the crowded city to build new factories; the postwar exodus to the new communities north of 8 Mile Road had begun long before a divisive figure like Coleman Young became mayor in the mid-1970s. As we saw in the introduction, sprawl is the natural condition of cities today, particularly in America. And today that process of creating a new urban form—lower density, powered by the private automobile—is all but complete in metropolitan Detroit. Tens of millions of square feet of new suburban office space sprouted like toadstools near highway exits in the '80s and '90s; suburban shopping malls grew larger, more upscale, and more distant from the old city center. Each year from the 1980s through the mid-2000s, suburban homebuilders added another ten thousand to fifteen thousand new houses, condos, and apartments to Detroit's suburban outer ring. Back in the older central city, all but stripped clean by decades of deindustrialization and white flight, a handful of new projects went up, heavily subsidized by a roster of redevelopment boards and agencies. But the real action continued to be in the suburbs.

By 2012, as I write this, the Detroit suburbs have become the city, in any real sense. As we saw in the introduction, only six percent of the taxable value of real estate in the tri-county Detroit area can be found in the city itself, while ninety-four percent is out in the suburbs. Let that statistic sink in. If we total up the dollar value of all the real estate on which the owners pay property taxes— all the homes and malls and office buildings and factories—today ninety-four cents of every dollar of that value is found in the suburbs; only six cents of every dollar of tax base is found in the city. Drive along major suburban arteries like Telegraph Road or Big Beaver or Rochester Road, and you pass seemingly endless shopping districts and housing developments and office and industrial parks. Die-hard Detroiters might disparage it all as inauthentic; one civic leader, in a private conversation with me, once called suburban sprawl "mile after mile of crapola." The aesthetics of suburbia aside, there's no denying that the city has largely been rebuilt out there beyond 8 Mile Road, the city's northern border.

Yet the outsiders who sniff that nobody lives in Detroit anymore face a comeuppance. Detroit remains among the top twenty cities in terms of population even today (although perhaps not for much longer); the city's population density, as we've seen earlier, is twice that of places like Phoenix and Dallas. My youngest brother, living in suburban Chicago, tells me that when he mentions to friends that I live in Detroit, they invariably ask, "In what suburb?" That someone with a job and means to move would voluntarily live in what many outsiders think of as an urban hell mystifies and astounds them.

So what do we make of Detroit after all these years? As a starting point, let's consider the 1960s-era documentary *City on the Move*, produced as part of Detroit's bid (unsuccessful) to host the 1968 Summer Olympic Games. The film highlighted the city's many assets—its humming auto factories, its bustling expressways—and it included a clip of President John F. Kennedy endorsing the bid. As an example of hubris before a fall, it's hard to beat: the city was seeping jobs and population even then, and the film (still available on the Web) boasted of Detroit's model race relations not long before race riots ripped the city asunder and sent thousands of families fleeing to the suburbs. Yet viewing the film with hindsight today, the most remarkable thing about *City on the Move* is not its outdated optimism but rather how much of what it portrayed remains valid. Case in point: the filmmakers touted the city's great center of learning, Wayne State University, along with Detroit's magnificent cultural institutions and its world-class hospitals; and of course those anchor institutions are still in business today, and in fact operate bigger and busier than ever. The Tigers and Red Wings still contend, the riverfront is more accessible to residents than ever, and the city's residents remain a passionate, deeply committed bunch.

This is not to say that all is fine in Detroit, as even a fleeting glance blows away any such notion. Detroiters may cringe at the media's portrayal of their city as an urban dystopia, but the image of Rust Belt failure is, of course, deserved. Detroit bleeds from a thousand wounds, and no happy talk will make that any less obvious or any less painful.

My point is to state the obvious: that Detroit is many cities today, a place of thriving neighborhoods yet abysmal abandonment; a city of highly educated professionals that is filled with illiterate dropouts; a city of soaring achievement in medicine, the arts, and industry, yet a city that paradoxically presents the most dispiriting vistas in urban America. No one vision or book or film or speech or exhibit or political agenda can capture the whole of Detroit today.

This is not quite the same as saying that any and all portrayals of Detroit are equally valid; merely that Detroit today stands as among the most complex urban environments in the world, absolutely unique in many ways. To truly understand this city, one needs to look beyond the boosterism of *City on the Move* but also beyond the ruin porn of so many current portrayals. Even after nearly twenty-five years covering this city as a journalist, I still learn new things about Detroit every day.

Photographers flock to this city today, along with journalists, academics, urban planners, sociologists, indeed anyone with an interest in the globe's great urban story of the early twenty-first century: What will happen to Detroit? True, many of the visitors come just to feast on the carcass of a once-great city, photographing wreckage and tut-tutting over the city's ills. But many people come to observe a new city being born. Listen to these visitors and you'll hear them say things like "Detroit is the new Berlin," meaning a city that will rise from the ashes (it's been done before, here) and re-create itself as a vibrant metropolis. Some believe Detroit will teach the world how a city can grow greener and more environmentally sustainable by producing much of its own food and energy, to a degree unknown around the world and that other cities will emulate. Others envy Detroit's opportunity to create new governance models to replace what is basically a nineteenth-century structure for governing large urban areas.

There's no certainty Detroit will implement any of this new thinking. Detroit's half-century fall from grace may continue, adding new chapters to that dreary saga of riots and redlining, white flight and suburban sprawl, shuttered factories, broken dreams, and wasted lives. But the opportunity to grow into a smaller but better city is real. Detroit has a chance, as Faulkner said of mankind, to not only endure but prevail.

Begin with the assets. Even in its distressed state, Detroit today remains home to about seven hundred thousand residents, ranking Detroit among the country's twenty largest cities. General Motors, one of the world's major manufacturers, calls the city home, while Ford is based nearby and Chrysler has significant assets in the area, too. Detroit's location at the most strategic spot on the entire Great Lakes offers the same critical advantages that French entrepreneurs saw in 1701. The city boasts world-class medical facilities, a major research institution in Wayne State University, historic architecture, excellent road and airport facilities, and a populace that remains passionate about their sports, their music, and their city.

But this tallying of assets does little of soften the drumroll of dreary statistics. Detroit has lost more than sixty percent of it population since its 1950s peak (1.8 million in 1950 to 713,777 at the 2010 census). The city's public schools rate at or near the bottom of all the nation's urban school districts. The official unemployment rate hovers around twenty percent as I write this in early 2012, but the unofficial estimates, once we include discouraged workers who have stopped trying or never started to look, run to twice that. Poverty remains among the worst in the nation. Much of the city's former population has picked up and moved to the suburbs. Today only about fourteen percent of the metropolitan region's jobs are found in Detroit itself, and the percentage is still declining. Surveyors have tallied more than 90,000 vacant residential parcels in the city— about one-quarter of all housing parcels. Estimates of vacant land in the city run as high as forty square miles once parks that are no longer tended and roads filled with dumped tires in abandoned neighborhoods are added to the vacant lots. That would amount to a swath of urban prairie into which the entire city of Paris, France, could be dropped.

The people who inhabit the Detroit of today defy easy characterization. The city is largely African American but holds significant populations of whites and Latinos, immigrants from multiple nations of the Middle East, and others. Detroit ranks among the nation's poorest cities, yet enjoys pockets of elegance and

Vacancy and abandonment in Detroit. (Author photo)

If put together, Detroit's vacant land would roughly equal the size of Paris, France. (Author photo)

districts of thriving cosmopolitanism. Any portrayal of Detroiters today captures at best a sampling.

So let's contrast two neighborhoods of many in Detroit—Midtown and Brightmoor—two districts that capture better than any the promise and the problems of Detroit.

The name "Midtown" for the district north of downtown Detroit started showing up in media accounts fairly recently, in the 1990s or so. Before that, the district between the northern edge of downtown and the New Center area about two miles to the north went by various names—the "Cultural Center" for the area around the Detroit Institute of Arts, the "Cass Corridor" for the big street west of Woodward, known mostly as a low-rent hangout for urban pioneers and aging '60s activists. But in recent years Midtown has emerged as Detroit's version of a combined college town and arts district with a cool urban vibe. Apartment buildings carry waiting lists; creative young people hoping to get in on the action often complain that they can't find a moderately priced place to live. New restaurants and shops seem to open weekly; abandoned apartment buildings undergo renovations; vacant lots see new uses.

Midtown's success stems, first and foremost, from the presence of major anchors—Wayne State, the Detroit Institute of Arts, Detroit Medical Center, the central branch of the Detroit Public Library, and more. These anchors and others bring close to thirty thousand workers a day into the Midtown area, while the growing network of art galleries, coffee shops, retail boutiques, and private residential developments bring many more. If downtown Detroit is recovering some of its corporate mojo, and Southwest Detroit enjoys a growing Latino immigration, Midtown Detroit is the place to find the young creative people who come to Detroit because it represents America's next urban village, its joys celebrated on Facebook, its good news carried far and wide by Twitter, a place where individuals still make a difference and where you can see positive change happening day by day.

Wayne State University, long a commuter school, started building high-rise dormitories around 2000, aiming to become more of a residential campus; each year, it seems, another dorm opens, and WSU rooms in Midtown now total in the several thousands, adding to the 24/7 atmosphere. The nearby College for Creative Studies, offering training in all types of art and design, took over an old General Motors building in New Center to expand its campus and created a hub of creativity where hundreds of students gather daily. Long-time private developers continued their patient renovations of derelict buildings. Perhaps most important, the district's main nonprofit group, formerly the University Cultural Center Association and now known as Midtown Detroit Inc., grew ever more skilled at attracting and leveraging dollars from foundations and the area's anchor universities and hospitals to promote new development, better urban design, and branding and marketing.

Besides the students, Midtown attracts many young professionals who see Detroit as the next great urban story, their place to make an impact while still young. Of the many of these we could highlight, let's meet Matthew Piper, a librarian by profession who chose Midtown as his field of action. Piper, who was twenty-seven when I spoke with him in early 2012, grew up in the outer suburbs of metro Detroit, and like many young people couldn't wait to move to another city. But as he earned a master's degree in library science at Wayne State University, he came to enjoy Midtown's energy and creativity and its evolving sense of place. "I had this click moment," he told me. "There's so much great stuff happening here, why would I go anywhere else?"

Piper met Tom and Peggy Brennan, founders of a new Midtown enterprise called the Green Garage. Carved out of a former Model T automobile service center and showroom, the Green Garage attempts to provide a laboratory for all sorts of sustainable ideas and technologies, like its porous "green alley" outside where permeable pavers and native gardens absorb excess rainwater. The Brennans and their friends mounted solar panels on the roof to heat water running through pipes under the floorboards to warm the building, used drywall made from ninety percent recycled materials, and reused doors from empty buildings across Detroit. (My newspaper, the *Detroit Free Press*, awarded the Green Garage one of its inaugural Michigan Green Leaders awards in 2010.) Piper offered to help the Brennans develop a library of urban sustainability ideas and sources. The library stocks some books, as in a traditional library, but mostly Piper connects people with others who can help them develop their greening projects. If someone needs, say, cheap cinder blocks to help build raised beds in a community garden, the sustainability library puts them in touch with people who have them.

"There's no book about that," Piper said. "The community becomes the collection rather than a collection of items. . . . We've had this remarkable freedom to do something new."

The spirit of innovation, that sense of Detroit being where it's happening right now, is pervasive in Midtown. "I think it's very valuable and very rare," Piper said. "I don't think you could find it in a lot of other places."

Much of the credit for the success of Midtown goes to Sue Mosey, the longtime leader of Midtown Detroit Inc. When she joined the then-named UCCA a quarter century ago, after graduating as an urban planner from Wayne State and spending a few years working in Southwest Detroit, she was one of a handful of paid staffers at her organization. Today, Mosey commands a paid staff of about twenty, with more hires on the way; the organization has added capacity and skills in real-estate development, urban design, and marketing. Foundations eager to back a winner in urban America have contributed millions of dollars to Midtown Detroit Inc. and its predecessor organization. So skilled

Tom and Peggy Brennan, founders and leaders of the Green Garage in Detroit's Midtown district, a showcase of environmentally sustainable practices and technologies. (Author photo)

at pulling the wires of urban renewal has Mosey become that Midtown is sometimes known among insiders as "Moseyville" and she herself "the mayor of Midtown." She notched a major victory in 2011 when Whole Foods Market Inc. agreed to open its first Detroit store in Midtown; it seemed to solidify her district's reputation as the city's coolest, most vibrant area.

Mosey readily admits that much remains to be done, and that change comes slowly—painfully slowly—in a city as disinvested as Detroit. New residential developments in Midtown, like the fifty-eight-unit, twelve-million-dollar Auburn project she broke ground on in 2011, still require a bevy of tax-credit incentives to make them economically feasible. The market, among the strongest in Detroit, remains far from "strong."

"You have to put things in perspective," Mosey told an interviewer for a 2012 article. "Everything is not going to happen in a short time period, but as long as you're moving forward . . . the neighborhood improves."

In an interview with me in the fall of 2011, she elaborated on that theme.

Susan Mosey, AKA "The Mayor of Midtown," for twenty-five years has led the revival of the city's university, cultural, and hospital district. (Author photo)

"It's rewarding every day to work in a city like Detroit," Mosey told me. "It's a challenging city in a lot of ways, but it is also a city of tremendous opportunity and tremendous people, and that keeps me going every day. To see the kind of interest and vibrancy coming back into this corridor is really, really rewarding."

And then there is Brightmoor, a district on the far west side of the city of Detroit. With its gently undulating topography bordering the meandering Rouge River, the independent town of Brightmoor remained farmland well into the early twentieth century. Then developers saw that the town stood near enough to Henry Ford's growing empire in nearby suburban Dearborn to offer a natural setting for worker housing. Detroit soon grew up and absorbed Brightmoor.

Among the developers taking advantage of the opportunity was one B. E. Taylor, who understood that many of the Ford workers would be coming up from Appalachia or the Deep South and were used to living in shacks; so Taylor provided worker cottages that sometimes had dirt floors and lacked indoor plumbing or electricity. Brightmoor's population stood at eight in 1922 but by 1925 had soared to more than eleven thousand. Ken Wolfe, a forty-year Brightmoor resident and local historian I spoke with in early 2012, described the newcomers as desperate men for whom sharecropping no longer put enough food on their families' tables; they worked for Ford until they had saved enough to bring up their women and children, often adding rooms onto their shacks as well as indoor plumbing and electricity. Infill homes built in later decades added to the mix, with the best homes nestled along the Rouge River and the city's Eliza Howell Park. As late as the 1970s, when Ken Wolfe moved in, Brightmoor was a mostly white working-class enclave with a strong memory of its farming heritage, a tight-knit neighborhood where every lot held a house, the owner of which kept his tiny plot well tended.

Today a drive through Brightmoor shows what forty years of white flight, disinvestment, a lack of city services, unrestrained dumping of trash, and financial collapse will do. Within about a fifteen-square block section at the core of Brightmoor, most of the homes are gone; driveway cutouts on narrow twenty-five-foot lots lead to nowhere; trash dumped by outsiders mars hundreds of lots; blighted trees and unkempt fields show nature trying to take over. Of the area's remaining structures, many are boarded up, or half collapsed from fire damage

Slows Bar-B-Q in Detroit has come to symbolize the commitment of the young and the hip to reinventing the city. (Author photo)

Corktown dates to the mid-1800s and remains a vibrant urban enclave even today. (Author photo)

or stripping. Thieves used to go after the copper piping and other metals with scrap value; lately they've been removing sections of vinyl siding from the remaining houses. Driving past one shuttered social-service agency, Wolfe remarks, "It's pretty bad when the Salvation Army moves out."

Wolfe himself owns a dozen properties in Brightmoor and takes pride in being a "resident landlord," one who counts his tenants as his neighbors and who works to keep up his properties—a breed growing increasingly rare in a city devastated by absentee landlords and speculators. Wolfe himself suggests that Brightmoor—and Detroit—are beyond help. He mentions a suggestion that has made the rounds—that the city bulldoze the rest of his neighborhood, dam the Rouge River to create "Lake Brightmoor," and sell the whole area to a nearby suburb. It's a sign of how far Brightmoor has fallen that even a committed resident like Wolfe doesn't find such ideas so farfetched.

Since the late 1980s, citizen activists in Brightmoor and the neighboring Old Redford district to the north have fought a long rear-guard action against blight, winning some key victories. John George, founder of the local group Blight Busters, gave up a career in insurance to start rehabbing houses in the

Once a tight-knit residential district for Ford workers, Brightmoor has come to symbolize abandonment in Detroit. (Author photo)

district in 1988, starting with a drug house operating next door to his own. As George recalled in one of our conversations in 2012, "I like a good party, but you don't piss in the bushes, you don't park on the lawn, you don't throw bottles in the street, you don't shoot guns in the air." George says he called the mayor's office, the police, the city council, the city's ombudsman, but nobody would do anything. So finally he boarded up the drug house himself, hauled away trash, and cut the grass, and when the drug dealers returned, they took one look and got back in their SUV and drove off. In the years since, George and his numerous volunteers have demolished, repaired, or built more than a thousand houses (earning George a visit to "The Oprah Winfrey Show," where the queen of daytime talk shows presented him with a cherry-red Volkswagen Beetle as a reward for his hard work).

So even in its distressed state, Brightmoor is not without its heroes, and we'll meet more of them later in this book. But one can celebrate their successes only so much. A drive through the wreckage of some parts of Brightmoor today can dim the spirits of the most optimistic urban enthusiast.

John George (left), the founder of Detroit's Blight Busters, and his chief gardener, Kofi Royal, have plans to keep expanding their community garden by acquiring vacant lots nearby. (Author photo)

We'll return to this district later. For now, though, suffice it to say that when outsiders contend that Detroit is beyond help and hope, districts like Brightmoor are what they mean.

"The economic forces that started this process were in place in the '40s," former Detroit City Council member Sheila Cockrel told me in 2011. "Stop and think about it. In 1961, when Jerry Cavanaugh became mayor, Detroit was seen as an all-American city. Detroit was the engine for the American economy. [But] he [Cavanaugh] had a six and a half million deficit. Why? Because the automobile industry had begun its migration out to the suburbs in the '40s." People who blame Detroit's first African American mayor, Coleman A. Young, for his confrontational style miss the point that Cockrel is making: suburban sprawl was well underway by the time Young was elected in 1974.

By now, that drain from the city is so complete that city government is broke, large swaths of the city lie empty and abandoned, and even the pockets of vitality feel the stress of encroaching vacancy. At any given time, an estimated twenty percent of the streetlights in the city don't work, plunging entire neighborhoods into the dark. Large parts of the city appear to be virtually ungoverned, as evidenced by the squatters who move into empty homes and the criminal stripping of metal and other salvageable items from thousands of buildings. In the Oakwood Heights neighborhood in far southwest Detroit, one woman told me that the police response to 911 calls proved so slow that when a squad car drives through the neighborhood children ask the police if they're lost.

If ever a city needed to reinvent its reason for being, it's Detroit. But Cockrel told me that many in the city, including her former colleagues on city council, are not yet ready to face that reality.

"For me, the typical debate in the city has devolved to a conversation about victimization and entitlement and race that absolutely misses the core point, which is, it's about the economy, the economy, the economy, jobs, jobs, jobs," she said. "What are we really doing today to prepare Detroiters for jobs that exist now or jobs that are coming in the future?"

It may help to remember that Detroit's story neatly falls into roughly hundred-year spans. The colonial period kicked off in 1701 when Cadillac stepped ashore from his canoe on the banks of the strait (*detroit* in French) and claimed this strategic outpost of the Great Lakes for France. A century of farming and fur trading, battles with Chief Pontiac's warriors and a generation-long rule by the British came to a symbolic end in 1805 when the wilderness outpost burned to the ground. Enter Judge Augustus Woodward and Detroit's second great century, a period in which the city blossomed into a financial center for the lumber and mining industries, relics of which can still be seen in architectural marvels like the Whitney Restaurant on Woodward Avenue and the Old Wayne County Building, both built with pre-automotive lumber fortunes. This nineteenth-century Detroit thrived as a center of shipbuilding and stove-making and railroad car manufacturing and, almost incredibly, tobacco processing. This era, too, came to an abrupt end, not by a conflagration but by the fiery emergence of a new industry that soon swept away everything in its path.

Detroit's Auto Century lasted, one might say, until 2009, when GM and Chrysler filed for bankruptcy and even the most upbeat had to admit that the auto companies would never again dominate as they once did. But during that automotive era Detroit flourished as few cities ever had. With factories swelling with production, Detroit enjoyed a tidal inflow of workers from all over the world, and the city burst its boundaries, annexing huge swathes of nearby communities to reach its current borders in the 1920s. The tiny village of Highland Park grew from four hundred residents in 1900 to four thousand in 1910 and then to forty thousand in 1920. Detroit ranked as the nation's thirteenth-largest city in 1900 and its fourth largest a mere twenty years later. The city's industrial powerhouses achieved prodigious feats of output, leading America to victory in World War II. Before the war, the entire nation produced no more than a few dozen tanks for the army; once Detroit retooled for the war effort, a single factory here turned out seven hundred tanks a month. At its peak, Ford's Willow Run bomber plant produced 650 B-24s every thirty days by 1944. In the great postwar boom, when America was the only nation left standing, the contentious union-management struggles in Detroit were mostly about dividing up the spoils of near-monopoly reach. It couldn't last, of course. Other nations would rebuild, learn to compete. Detroit, sadly, ignored the competition as long as it could, until long after it was time to do something.

This long, slow post-war period of industrial slippage coincided with the great out-migration from our cities to nearby villages and towns. Certainly the automotive companies played a part lobbying for new suburban roads; so did federal and state subsidies for suburban growth; and so did consumer choice, as people willingly traded city streets and public transportation for big backyards and attached garages. Detroit is hardly alone in suffering big losses to the suburbs, but no city emptied out more than Detroit, as today's empty landscapes in the city bear witness. The loss of the city's manufacturing base left huge gaps in the city's landscape. So, too, did the loss of population, as jobs went elsewhere and workers found they could afford homes in the new, less crowded suburbs to the north and west.

A city that prided itself on offering the nation's highest level of home ownership to blue-collar workers now found that those simple wood-frame bungalows didn't hold up well to abandonment and vandalism. As the city demolished thousands of empty houses to eradicate blight, the cityscape we see today began to emerge, that strange mix of vibrant neighborhoods like Indian Village and mile upon mile of rural-like vacancy. Other cities lost industry, too, but often their lost industries occupied smaller footprints than Detroit's giant factories, and their solid brick tenement housing for workers held up better in the post-war years than Detroit's bungalows. And so we see the city as it exists today—a city suffering so much vacancy that it stands as the international symbol of urban ills.

It has become an article of faith among many that Detroit's vacancy and abandonment, viewed for so long as a calamity and a shame, now creates Detroit's opportunity for greatness. Not everyone agrees, of course, and doubters see this line of optimistic thinking as just another mirage. Nonetheless, new urban thinkers of all stripes are heading to Detroit today from all over the world because of that perceived opportunity. Detroit, the nation's most abandoned big city, stands ready to serve as the world's biggest laboratory for trying out new urban ideas.

So what are these new urban ideas? For a time in Detroit, it appeared that single-shot solutions might suffice—urban gardening here, casino gaming there, and a dollop of better race relations. But the municipal crisis in America has gone too far. Half measures won't do. With our legacy cities drained of tax

Two common sights today in Detroit: A farmstand at a community garden, and a filmmaker documenting it. (Author photo)

base, municipal governments no longer work. With steel and auto production gone, urban unemployment creates a permanent underclass. With thousands of square miles of older urban America slowly returning to nature, pockets of urban America have become ghost cities.

Fortunately, a lot of smart people in a lot of distressed cities have been working on this. They have been willing, as Abraham Lincoln urged in a dark hour, to think anew and act anew. The balance of this book will look at their solutions.

NEW WAYS TO GOVERN OUR CITIES

THE UNIVERSITY CIRCLE STORY

On the afternoon of May 9, 2003, a former graduate student named Biswanath Halder, sixty-two, wearing a wig, helmet, and bulletproof vest, smashed through a glass door at Case Western Reserve University in Cleveland. Once inside, Halder shot the first three people he saw, wounding two and killing a thirty-year-old MBA student from Youngstown named Norman Wallace. Halder kept scattering shots as students and faculty ran or barricaded themselves in offices. Police arrived, and there was a sharp exchange of gunfire. Halder took advantage of the curvy walls and hidden recesses of the Frank Gehry–designed Peter B. Lewis Building to slip deeper into the interior. But the near-immediate arrival of the police had forced Halder into a defensive posture; and instead of a Virginia Tech–style massacre with dozens dead, the only other person wounded was Halder himself, who hid in a closet during a seven-hour standoff before finally surrendering to police. He later told authorities he did not know the people he shot; he was upset at another person in the building who had hacked into his Web site for entrepreneurs from India. Convicted of multiple counts, he received a sentence of life without parole.

A tragedy, and one that could have swelled into something much more horrible; but the rampage also lets us glimpse something important about how municipal governance may be evolving today. The first responders to enter the building were police officers named Staff Sergeant Kenji Kurokawa and Sergeant Daniel Stein. They wore the uniforms and badges not of the Cleveland city police, nor the Cuyahoga County Sheriff's SWAT team, nor the nearby suburban Euclid police, nor the FBI, all of which responded during the seven-hour siege. Instead, they served as members of the University Circle Police Department, a unit formed by and reporting to a nonprofit community group called University

Circle Inc., which operates, if not as a mini-government, then certainly as a significant overseer of a square-mile chunk of Cleveland's east side. UCI gets its name from the neighborhood itself, a district that dates to the 1800s and is now home to not only Case Western but a cluster of other schools, hospitals, and museums; it is one of America's many Eds-and-Meds-and-Arts districts, roughly equivalent to Detroit's Midtown district. Of course, numerous well-to-do neighborhoods in American cities hire private security firms to patrol their streets, and colleges and corporations often have their own security forces; but rare is the nonprofit community organization that operates a police force, armed and with full arrest powers, under contract with the municipal government and wielding an array of municipal-like powers.

Chris Ronayne, a former mayoral chief of staff and chief development officer for Cleveland and now president of UCI, told me during my visit in mid-2011 that the organization acts more and more as a small-scale city government for its district: "We cut the lawns on the public realm, we maintain the public parks here in the district, we sweep the sidewalks, we deal with graffiti abatement, we're the eyes and ears on the street with hospitality advisers. We are also the marketing arm for this part of the city. We're one part community development corporation, one part special improvement district, and one part chamber of commerce."

And, he added, their police force does everything from rescue cats from trees to confront lunatic gunmen.

In the introduction and chapter one, we saw that the tax base of many great cities has mostly fled to the suburbs. Detroit today, as mentioned, holds only six percent of its regional tax base, a sliver that is too little to generate the kind of revenue needed to operate a full range of municipal services over Detroit's 139 square miles. The City of Cleveland's plight is not quite so dire, but almost: Cleveland today contains just twelve percent of its regional tax base, and the meager resources that provides has had Cleveland officials nipping and tucking almost as desperately as Detroit's elected leaders. It is this book's contention that our cities have mostly moved beyond the point of no return here; that no amount of cutting can fix the municipal corporations that run our cities, or bring them back to a state of fiscal health. And so we need to evolve some new ways for our cities to govern themselves, and these new ways must be truly creative.

They cannot be mere extensions of what we're doing already— relying on state or federal government to bail out strapped municipal governments; appointing fiscal dictators ("emergency managers") to implement draconian cuts on municipal salaries and benefits; or, on the other hand, continuing to abandon our cities to the weeds and the outlaws.

Americans were brilliant in inventing modern democratic government during the late eighteenth century, but we're generally unable or unwilling to reinvent government now to meet modern needs. That the regional Detroit area now boasts more than 250 units of government speaks to the problem. Those are cities, villages, townships, and counties, not to mention numerous school districts and special taxing authorities, and it's hard to see how metro Detroit's long-suffering populace is well served by hundreds of mayors, town councils, and multiples of everything else. Michigan alone has 550 public school districts, which is more, I've been told, than exist in all of Western Europe. There must be a better way.

In this chapter, we'll explore some of those better ways. And one way we can improve municipal governance is to break off pieces of municipal government and send those tasks either "upstream" (as in the regional transportation authorities that operate city-and-suburban transit systems in many metro areas) or "downstream" to neighborhood-level groups that can handle them better. We already do that to a certain extent, of course, in many cities. But we could do a lot more. And perhaps no downstream group shows the way better than University Circle Inc.

The district takes it name not only from the universities that call it home but also from a traffic circle in the heart of it all. Located four miles east of downtown Cleveland, University Circle grew from the late nineteenth century onward from a small settlement into a world-class assemblage of education, health care, and arts institutions. The spark came in the late 1800s when two universities in Cleveland—Western Reserve University and Case Institute of Technology— sought to relocate to an area with enough room to grow. Many more followed: the Western Reserve School of Design for Women (Cleveland Institute of Art) by the 1890s; the Cleveland Museum of Art in 1916; University Hospitals in 1931; plus a score of others, from the Cleveland Botanical Garden to the Cleveland Museum of Natural History.

A dense concentration of Eds and Meds and Arts like this proves a boon to almost any city that enjoys it; look no farther than Detroit's Midtown district to see how anchors employ thousands of smart, well-paid professionals who like to eat, shop, live, and play in a walkable urban environment. The anchors operate as nonprofits, and so contribute no property taxes to a municipality like Cleveland (a growing source of irritation, as we saw earlier), but they contribute enormously by providing good jobs and a cultural significance indispensible to a city's image and morale.

University Circle Inc. itself grew from a philanthropic effort in 1950 into a quest to knit together the thirty-four different institutions in the district through better urban planning. That led to adoption in the late '50s of the University Circle Master Plan, which, in broad terms, envisioned enhancing the parks and other public spaces while developing available land with a prudent eye toward the overall good of the district. This master plan set a goal to "establish a central organization to administer the plan and give it some real authority." That recommendation gave birth to the University Circle Development Foundation, which quickly formed a land bank to buy and hold available land until one or another institution needed it for expansion. Other services soon followed: police, parking, shuttle buses, architectural design review, landscaping of common areas. In 1970, the UCDF was reorganized as University Circle Inc. and charged by its directors to explore stronger relationships with surrounding neighborhoods, some of which were among the poorest in Ohio. By the 1970s, UCI was helping to found schools for Cleveland schoolchildren; by the '90s, it was morphing from a passive holder for the district's excess land to a promoter, developer, and catalyst for historic renovation and construction of commercial and residential properties.

Today, it's almost easier to list what UCI doesn't do than what it does. It takes bids from developers to build on vacant land in and near the district. It is talking with adjoining suburbs, most of which are poor and struggling, about UCI providing police patrols, street cleaning, and business services like recycling or selling office supplies at group discounts for a fee.

"We run this corporation as if it's a small suburb," Ronayne says.

To me, the most striking illustration of how groups like UCI operate as what I might call "quasi-municipal entities" came the day Chris Ronayne drove me around the district during a late 2011 visit. As Ronayne pointed out, the streets we drove on—the responsibility for which still rests with Cleveland's city government—showed the most wear and tear, the pavement pitted, chipped, or potholed in places, while everything else—maintained by UCI and its crews—presented a neat, trim, even immaculate appearance. Curb to curb on the streets, the realm of the underfunded municipal government, the urban environment might look rutted or uneven; but UCI under contract with the city kept everything else looking like a postcard image of a busy, walkable district.

"We don't rely on the city to keep it clean, safe, and attractive. We rely on ourselves," Ronayne said.

Every bump in the road that day brought home to me the sorry state of municipal finances; remember, the City of Cleveland accounts for just twelve percent of its regional tax base. Too few dollars coming into the city coffers mean too little upkeep to city streets; while UCI, with a surer, if modest, revenue stream from district institutions, could not only keep the district clean and well-maintained but do real-estate development, create way-finding signage, conduct destination-marketing campaigns, and operate a police force.

"These Eds-Meds-Arts districts are kind of self-sufficient," Ronayne told me that day. "Have they been doing what the government should otherwise do? Probably. Have they done it despite the government not doing it? Yes. Why? Because if we didn't do it, nobody would do it. That's the truth in this town."

That's the truth in so many towns. Perhaps the time has come to stop looking at groups like UCI as a backstop for weak or nonexistent city services and more as a model for a new way of governing urban places. These hyper-local, government-like bodies might be combined with regional entities—some of which may not even exist yet—to provide flexible, efficient delivery of services. Ronayne, for one, is already thinking along these lines:

> The new construct is less federal-state-local and more neighborhood-regional-global. I would envision a day when we're given the rights to tamp potholes and maintain basic infrastructure, to plow streets. Now, can we mill, fill, and build new streets? No, that's a whole other dynamic. But in this era, you're going to see groups like ours grow in municipal services. Now, some people argue that [by] providing the service, you're giving the city an out. I don't, as a former chief of staff, look at it that way. I

look at it as somebody's got to get the job done, and however it can get done most economically and efficiently, let's do it.

As if to echo that, city officials in Detroit admitted in early 2012 that the city's Human Services Department could no longer manage the federal early childhood education program known as Head Start and would tell the federal government to stop sending the fifty million dollars a year to the city for that program. The problem: an environment of nepotism, reckless spending, and corruption in local management of Head Start.

"Mayor [Dave Bing]'s administration has decided that it is in the best interest of the residents if DHS does not apply for Head Start funds," Loretta Davis, group executive of the city's health and human services, told the *Detroit Free Press*. "This decision is based on the administration's belief that some programs operate more efficiently outside of city government." The US Department of Health and Human Services would seek applicants from other governments and nonprofits to take over administering the Head Start money, which is used to help children of lower-income families prepare for school. As the *Free Press* pointed out, the local program was the target of criticism over waiting lists, dirty and dangerous classrooms, and no-bid contracts. "It's a big mess," said Aries Davis, a member of the Detroit Head Start Policy Committee, which oversees program spending. "No one has been accountable to anyone. Since we aren't seeing any progress, I'm happy that the city is losing the money. Someone else needs to run Head Start."

Ronayne, as a former mayoral chief of staff with finely tuned political instincts, knows better than to draw too sharp a contrast between his organization's success and Cleveland's municipal failures. But other activists in other positions are not so reluctant. Take, for example, John George, the founder and head of the Blight Busters organization in Detroit's Brightmoor district whom we met earlier. George, like many Detroit activists, seems willing to talk all day about the failures of city government—to return phone calls, to process grant applications in a timely manner, to simply get out of the way of neighborhood-level work. Noting that some of the aid dollars that come to Blight Busters come from federal programs funneled through the city, George doesn't hide his frustration: "If the federal government has any money, it should go directly to organizations like Blight Busters, Habitat for Humanity, Northwest Detroit Neighborhood Development, U Snap Bac, New Hope Nonprofit Housing, Granmont-Rosedale. We're doing all the goddamn work. Why do we have this middleman in the way that's inefficient, wastes money, has no idea what to do?"

You can hear that sentiment echoed in many urban communities today, where on-the-ground activists bemoan the delays and inadequacies of municipal leadership. But it's hard for city governments to own up to their failures, to their chronic inability to deliver services as they should. And it's even more difficult—often agonizingly so—for these municipalities to transfer their ineptly run operations either "upstream" to regional organizations or "downstream" to groups like UCI that could run them better. Perhaps no episode so illustrates the difficulty of wresting control of failed municipal operations away from a city, or of the gains to be made by doing so, as the story of Detroit's Eastern Market.

THE EASTERN MARKET STORY

Jim Sutherland came to Eastern Market on a bitterly cold day in early January 2003, a day with the wind whistling through the market's open air sheds. Fresh from Professor Robin Boyle's urban planning class at Wayne State University, Sutherland had reported for duty as an intern with the civic group Downtown Detroit Partnership. Interns always get the scut work, tedious but sometimes important, and his new boss, Kate Beebe, a longtime urban planner in Detroit and at that time president of the civic partnership, gave him an assignment whose routine belied its significance.

Beebe and her organization, a group recently formed from the merger of two other nonprofit entities, were seeking an identity, a mission; rescuing the city's Eastern Market from decades of decline and neglect looked like it might make a good fit. The city's mayor, Kwame Kilpatrick, new to office and still full of promise, had visited the famed Pike Place Public Market in Seattle and came back brimming with enthusiasm. So at Beebe's direction Sutherland visited the market to start creating base maps—an inventory of the public infrastructure there—that would help everyone chart a new direction for the market.

Sutherland, today the market's vice president of operations, remembers that frigid day as the start of his romance with the market. With the temperatures

Detroit's Eastern Market shows what can happen when a poorly run city asset is turned over to a professionally managed nonprofit organization. (Courtesy of Eastern Market Corp.)

well below freezing, Sutherland and a co-worker measured every sidewalk, curb cut, telephone pole, and garage door in every shed, focusing mainly on the market core and the retail properties that faced Russell and Riopelle Streets.

Some background: As late as the 1960s, Eastern Market still thrived with shoppers and merchants of Polish and other white ethnic stock who lived in the city. Those same shoppers and their parents and grandparents had been coming to Eastern Market's stalls for decades to buy their potatoes and beets and peppers and seasonal fruits; they had been doing so dating back to 1891 when the city set up the market east of downtown (hence the name, and contrasted with a Western Market on the city's west side that was long since lost to urban renewal projects). Eastern Market actually consists of several sub-markets; there is the market proper, owned and run by the City of Detroit, consisting of several blocks of large market sheds, offering in all hundreds of stalls for farmers to display their produce. (Somewhat illogically, the market's five public sheds are numbered 2 through 6, the former Shed 1 having been lost to the construction of the I-75 expressway.) Today, on Saturday mornings, farmers from surrounding villages on the outskirts of Detroit truck in their goods, and thousands of shoppers throng the stalls. Surrounding this north-south row of market sheds, like a fringe of homes around a park, are private food businesses, everything from family-run general stores specializing in meats and cheeses and coffees and nuts, to butcher shops and meat-packers, plus restaurants and delis popular with both suburbanites and Detroit's emerging hip creative class. Finally, and in some ways most importantly, the market functions as a wholesale supplier of produce to grocery stores and restaurants; it's a seven-days-a-week operation where retailers back up their trucks to warehouse loading docks between midnight and dawn to stock up on the day's supplies.

"It's got kind of a soul to it," Fr. Norman Paul Thomas, the longtime pastor of the nearby Sacred Heart Church, says of Eastern Market. "There's a lot of character."

But, as Sutherland knew, by the 1990s Eastern Market, like public markets in many other cities, had grown more than a little shopworn. The Polish customer base had moved out to Macomb County, spurred by all the usual reasons for heading to the suburbs and one other reason in particular—the demolition of a largely Polish neighborhood in Detroit and Hamtramck in the early '80s to make way for General Motors' Poletown factory. That then-mayor Coleman A. Young could wipe an entire neighborhood of more than a thousand homes off the map told many of the city's remaining Poles they weren't welcome. Then, too, the vegetables and fruits available at the Saturday market for the public were no longer so fresh. Besides local farmers selling in the stalls, there were businessmen vendors who simply bought produce at the city's west-side terminal, where fruits and vegetables came in from all over the world, and sold them at the market. But these latter vendors often dumped overripe fruit and salad greens past their prime. "People started saying, 'I got cheated here,'" Fr. Thomas says. "We had meetings with vendors to make sure that they didn't sell junk yet still could make some money." But the junk continued to be sold, and sometimes, Sutherland adds, the attitude would be "take this from the terminal, get what you can for it, and then leave it out back of the sheds because the city will pay to dispose of it and it doesn't have to go into our dumpsters and we can cut our disposal bills."

At the heart of the problems lay the frustration with Detroit's ongoing decline, the loss of people and jobs that constricted the city's ability to give Eastern Market the attention it needed. The diminished police protection, the lack of city services, the inability or unwillingness to pay for normal upkeep at the market—all these took their toll. Bureaucracy at city hall, where control of Eastern Market shuffled from one department to another, proved debilitating. Sutherland told me of one business owner who struggled for years to buy a side lot next to his business so he could expand and add more jobs. And that was a city-owned parcel.

Yet for all that, the market still had a core of vitality. Many of the businesses, the meat-packers and wholesalers in particular, were too heavily invested in their equipment to easily move out. And the owners were stubborn. "There were strong personalities," Fr. Thomas says. "I really admired those guys, all those old-timers. They were strong, and because of that there were always clashes. But they loved the Eastern Market and they hung in there. I was amazed at how hard they worked."

Jim Sutherland quickly came to agree.

"There was still a huge passion for this place," he says. "I can shop in Kroger but that's a chore. This is an experience. It's about the food, but it's about something more. It was that sense of place. It was a lot of fun, maybe a little dangerous. That was part of the customer passion."

Some of the merchants at the market had asked the authoritative Project for Public Spaces in New York to look at the market in 1996, and Dave O'Neil, the head of the Project's public markets staff, came out for a visit. "I could see it just soon as I got there, it had so much potential," O'Neil said much later. "So it was really great to get involved with it." Around that same time Detroit's previous mayor, Dennis Archer, created a task force to look at the future of Eastern Market, asking Fr. Thomas to chair the effort, and Fr. Thomas recalls the endless meetings and visits to other cities and various plans drawn up, but that not much came of all the effort. The bureaucracy was too ossified, the merchants too divided, and the city was too understaffed and short of cash to pay much attention. Time passed. More studies were done. "I'm meeting'd to death," Fr. Thomas told me.

So when Jim Sutherland set out that frigid January morning to measure sidewalks and curb cuts, he could be excused for thinking, as he later said, "So here goes round four or ten depending on who you talk to."

There was this, though: all those previous studies had reached the same conclusion, that management of Eastern Market needed to go into a more nimble structure, away from direct city control.

"However you wanted to code it, that meant privatization, or taking it out of the hands of city management," Sutherland said much later. "Some people sugarcoated it more than others," he added, but it was clear to many that the market suffered by getting shuffled from city department to city department—finance or recreation or cultural affairs—always an unwanted stepchild for departments whose core focus lay elsewhere.

Sutherland soon learned that the market's human environment could prove even more complex than the physical infrastructure. Many of the white ethnic business owners who ran these wholesale suppliers had run their businesses for decades with a fierce and protective pride. Many of the old-time merchants in the shops and warehouses surrounding the market were feuding more or less all the time. Often the sparks were trivial but they fanned into flames all the same.

"Everyone had his own kingdom," Fr. Thomas says. "There were rivalries at times, some old hurts along the way. Some guy had his stuff out on the street. 'Well, why is he doing that? I have to pay for this and that, what's he get free street space for.' Stuff like that."

So against this background of economic decline and inbred feuds, Sutherland did his mapping and Kate Beebe hired the Gensler architectural firm to start to put some ideas on paper. Everyone knew that wresting control of Eastern Market away from city departments would be difficult. The city remained (and remains) fiercely protective of its "jewels" like the market. As Sutherland puts it today, "So we got to that and said, 'Hmmm, we're telling you, you have to privatize it.'" And then wait for the explosion.

Beebe, a veteran of the city's development wars, decided to go at it from another direction—from a design perspective—to come up with an arresting vision of what the market could look like once improved, get everyone jazzed up over that, and then try to figure out how to overcome the hurdle of city ownership and operational control.

In March 2003, Beebe formed a working group that included the leaders of the private merchants, the city's administration, and others. She hoped that the goal of a better market would carry everyone through the antagonisms that had built up over the years. "Even amongst the warring factions, it was pretty well understood that this was a place that people were highly passionate about, even though they bitched a lot. You got that positive energy," Sutherland says.

But for a while the human element looked pretty bleak. Market merchants had split into rival groups, one being the Eastern Market Merchants Association, led by a professional association representative named Ed Deeb, and the other the Eastern Market Advancement Coalition, led by a longtime merchant named Joe Kuspa. Deeb and Kuspa did not get along; at meetings of the working group, Sutherland says, they would sit at the table refusing even to look at each other. Added to the mix were three different municipal unions that were suspicious of Beebe's motives and worried about losing the small group of City of Detroit employees working at the market—not more than about six people at this time.

"So then you had the Italians aligned against the Chaldeans aligned against the farmers aligned against whatever other constituency you wanted to come up with," Sutherland says. "It was very much like the breakup of Yugoslavia around here."

But Beebe had one big card to play—money. Several foundations eager to help the city and interested in the burgeoning local food movement were willing to put in big money—some $4.5 million—if an appropriate new management control could be worked out. That motivated everyone to get along. The working group met for six months and came up with a general plan to take control of Eastern Market away from the city and give it to a nonprofit public authority. The foundation money—from the Kellogg Foundation, the McGregor Fund, and the Kresge Foundation—would fund everything.

But not quite yet. The Kilpatrick administration, which had to bless the whole thing and convince City Council to approve the privatization of the market, was losing interest for a time. There were other things going on—the city's attempt to redevelop the derelict Book-Cadillac Hotel (finally reopened in late 2008), and its ambitious cleanup of downtown for the Super Bowl XL extravaganza in February 2006. Everything on the Eastern Market front just sort of idled month after month. "We were sitting there saying how do we not get lost in this process," Sutherland said.

So Beebe came up with another stratagem. She brought in the Urban Land Institute, a national real estate forum with a strong Michigan presence, to conduct one of their intensive multiday planning exercises focusing on the market. George Jackson, president of the Detroit Economic Growth Corporation, who believed in the market reorganization, gave money from his funds for the ULI exercise, and others came up with cash, too, and the panel of outsiders met in December 2004. Everyone agreed the market was a gem badly in need of polishing. They drew up plans showing how the city's market sheds could be renovated to enhance the shopping experience and thus produce more jobs and tax revenue for the city.

"At end of it, Bill Lashbrook at PNC Bank said it best at the final presentation at Ford Field," Sutherland says. "'Hey guys, you've talked and you've talked and you've talked. You've had plans, you've had ideas. No more talk. Now's the time to do something. You've got money. You've got a plan. You've got a will. Do something.'"

Then there came one of those moments that signal a shift in terrain. Sutherland remembers seeing Walt Watkins, a retired banker serving as Kilpatrick's chief development officer, standing looking at one of the overall concept boards for the market, just standing there quietly pondering it, and Beebe came up and Watkins said something to her, and Beebe turned around and came over to Sutherland. She was very, very pleased. "He gets it," she said.

So in early 2005 the lawyers for Beebe's group and the city started to get serious about writing up the transfer plan to move the market from the city's direct control to a new Eastern Market Corporation, involving a professional staff to be overseen by a nonprofit board. They wrote a management agreement and bylaws. And, not least, the team was strategizing how to get it through a skeptical city council, which, then as now, looks askance at any privatization scheme, no matter how much sense it makes. So they drafted and redrafted and held meetings with Council members and staffs, and there were visits to other public markets around the nation to learn about operational structures. That consumed all of 2005 and part of 2006. Sutherland was learning the intricate political landscape of the city council, where distrust of outsiders ran strong and where Council members (some of them, anyway) feared a loss of support of municipal unions almost more than anything else. Opponents of the transfer, like the city municipal unions, used their contacts on Council to slow down the whole process. People weren't above spreading rumors and innuendos about those pushing for the new concept.

"There were a lot of internal machinations there," Sutherland says. "It got pretty ugly."

Kilpatrick himself favored the new plan, and his team (some of whom were later, like Kilpatrick himself, caught up in a corruption scandal) was working hard to get the plan through Council. Sutherland remembers that the final agreement before Council was the thirty-seventh version, but there were so many rewritings that no one really knew. They had an ally on the Council in Sheila Cockrel, who had a reputation of reading every last financial document that came before her and who was not afraid to embrace new ways to reinvent the city. Cockrel knew that the plan needed some political cover, had to be sold as a full public-private partnership, and couldn't look strictly like privatization, even if it was. So the City of Detroit would keep ownership of the market but cede virtually all control to the new market corporation.

Cockrel today, retired from city council and teaching at Wayne State University, remembers the debate as a tired repetition of past privatization stories.

"It's frustrating because the conversation became one of those, you know, 'Where do you live, who are you, this is a city jewel, we can't be giving away city jewels.' It was the wrong conversation," she told me.

The final debate, in June 2006, proved rancorous, with some Council members playing to the cameras and all the city's divisive animosities over race and loss of control hovering in the air. Beebe and her team agreed to retain four of the city workers then employed at the market. Even then the final vote was delayed. The Kresge Foundation forced the issue by giving the city a deadline to approve the transfer of control or otherwise lose its two-million-dollar grant. The Hudson-Weber Foundation was ready to give more money, and DTE Energy, the local power company, was lined up to donate in-kind services. With so much on the line, Council voted 6–3 in favor of the transfer, but there was a privatization ordinance on the books requiring at least a 7–2 vote, so Beebe and her team got one more extension from Kresge on the deadline and reworked the plan one more time that night. It passed the next day 8–1, with Council member Joann Watson, the panel's most vociferous defender of the rights of municipal workers, casting the lone "no" vote.

The transfer date was July 30, 2006, a Sunday, a little over a month later. Beebe would serve as interim president of the Eastern Market Corporation until a professional market manager could be hired.

So on Monday morning, July 31—the temperature and humidity both rising into the nineties that day—Beebe and her team showed up at the city's market headquarters to find that departing city employees had emptied the office. The place was cleaned out. All the records were gone—copies of leases with vendors, payrolls, purchasing and billing data, everything. The departing city workers had left only a huge pile of shredded documents. There wasn't even any air conditioning. Sutherland looked around and said, "Oh, shit." And he called his wife to ask her to go to Target and buy him a bunch of golf shirts and shorts and underwear. "I was like, 'I'm not going to have time to do laundry. I'll just throw it in the car and we'll sweat it out,'" he says.

During the more than three years spent preparing for that moment, the team had assembled a pretty good idea of how the market ran. And the next Saturday, as farmers and vendors set up in their stalls for the public market day, Sutherland and the others went from stall to stall to ask what sort of lease agreements everyone had with the market.

"Basically all we did was walk around and talk to the vendors and ask them what they paid and why," Sutherland says. "I had enough information I could kind of figure out where the truth lay. What was really bizarre about the leasing over there, there were thirty-eight different prices. Bizarre arrangements for different reasons." Whether these deals represented the fruits of payoffs for favors or special locations, nobody knew. But Sutherland now understood the truth of what an auditor, hired by the city a couple of years earlier, had written in his report on the market. "The report came back with the first line: 'The books of the market are unauditable. Just change things and move on,'" Sutherland recalled. And so they did.

The chaos diminished with time. Almost immediately the market began to show improvements. The Kellogg and Kresge foundations pumped in money, and work began on the renovations of the Sheds 2 and 3. Shed 2 remains an open-air, open-sided venue for Saturday market day, but Shed 3 morphed to a year-round venue for special events, from auto show previews to fashion shows to book launches. The renovation of Shed 3 cost six million dollars, paid for mostly with foundation money, and involved an all-new floor with radiant heating, new windows, upgrading the electrical systems, and shafts into the earth to create a geothermal heating and cooling system eventually. In December 2009, General Motors hosted journalists for an unveiling of new vehicles in the renovated Shed 3. Susan Docherty, GM's vice president of sales and marketing, marveled at the upgrades, the glass walls, and other changes that had transformed the decades-old shed.

"Boy, it felt like we could have been in New York or Boston with how terrific the renovations on that facility looked," she said. "It was a perfect location."

Beebe served as interim president until 2007, when the board hired Dan Carmody, a one-time tavern keeper turned economic development official, to run the new corporation. Carmody, a high-energy leader, encourages innovative thinking. Under his direction the market has flourished; occupancy of the market stalls has swelled from about sixty percent when the city ran the market to one hundred percent now. New product offerings began to show up in stalls—no longer could shoppers find just fruits and vegetables, but now there were more specialty food vendors selling grass-fed pork and beef, artisan breads and cheeses, coffees and teas, pierogies—those small pastries stuffed with meat and other tasty bits.

"We've come a long way in the last four years," said Ed Deeb, the longtime head of the Eastern Market Merchants Association who went on to serve on the market's board of directors.

In late 2011 work began on Shed 5's restoration with money from the Ford Foundation. The work includes creation of a community kitchen where local food entrepreneurs can book space by the hour to create products; there will also be cooking demonstrations and specialty classes. And the sidewalk area outside Shed 5 along Russell Street, the market's main street, will be converted to a public plaza for arts-and-crafts shows and other special events.

In 2011, the market began offering public market shopping on Tuesdays as well as Saturdays, part of a plan to eventually open the market at least two or three days a week year-round. And the market looks even beyond that. "We want this to be a six-or-seven-day-a-week market," Deeb told me.

I dwell at such length on the Eastern Market story because it illustrates so well how *pieces* of municipal government can work so much better if spun off into special-purpose entities—conservancies, authorities, quasi-public corporations, and the like. Many such bodies operate in Detroit now; one can make a pretty good case that anything good accomplished in the city lately has happened through one of these limited-purpose bodies. After decades of bemoaning the sorry state of the waterfront, Detroiters now enjoy strolling, bicycling, bird-watching, and other recreational activity on the splendid RiverWalk, a three-mile (one day to be as much as a 5.5-mile or even longer) riverfront promenade built in recent years by the nonprofit Detroit Riverfront Conservancy. Technically the City of Detroit owns the RiverWalk, but the conservancy, created in 2002, built and operates the promenade relatively free from city oversight; the Kresge Foundation donated fifty million dollars in a matching grant to pay for it, and General Motors (its headquarters located in the Renaissance Center on the riverfront) paid for most of the rest, with Matthew Cullen, then head of GM's real-estate development activities, co-chairing the conservancy's board. Then, too, Campus Martius Park, re-created at Detroit's historic city center (named for the military drilling that used to take place there in colonial days; the name is Latin for "Field of Mars") came about through the same sort of nonprofit conservancy. As an outgrowth of the city's three-hundredth anniversary in 2001, a nonprofit group known as the Detroit 300 Conservancy, headed by automotive heir Edsel Ford II, cast about for something of value to leave behind, and settled on revitalizing the long-dormant Campus Martius. As with the creation of the RiverWalk, the private conservancy board designed, built, and operates the park under contract with the city. Elsewhere, the city's magnificent Detroit Institute of Arts, its Historical Museum, and the Detroit Zoo all once languished under direct city control, and all now do better (if occasionally still facing budget challenges) managed by their own nonprofit, quasi-public boards.

One of the most dramatic turnarounds took place at Cobo Center, Detroit's riverfront convention facility. Cobo was so poorly run as a department of city government over the years that Detroit nearly lost its signature North American International Auto Show to other cities. Costs ran high, work rules were strangling, the roof even leaked. Finally, in late 2009, after years of divisive debate, the city agreed to let a new Detroit Regional Convention Facility Authority take control of Cobo. In barely two years, the new five-member authority (with appointees representing the city, the three regional counties, and the state) had hired professional management, begun a three-hundred-million-dollar multiyear expansion and upgrade, and signed a multiyear contract to host the auto show well into the future.

I was amazed as a reporter covering the city for two decades to see how quickly problems like Eastern Market and Cobo could turn around—indeed, how they could flourish and prosper—once out of the hands of the underfunded, understaffed Detroit city government. Reporters (and the public) often think we're witnessing trench warfare, where problems fester and nothing ever seems to improve. Eastern Market and Cobo give reason to hope.

Another lesson suggests itself from the Eastern Market story—that we can find the cash to improve our cities even though municipal governments themselves are broke. Detroiters improved the market and built the RiverWalk and Campus Martius Park, three projects that totaled more than one hundred million dollars, yet the city's treasury paid for virtually none of it, other than some routine staffing for legal work and other odds and ends. Foundations and corporations ponied up the great bulk of the money, tens of millions of dollars, and private donors contributed some more, and revenues from leasing market stalls or hosting special events at the venues helped cover operational costs. Indeed, most of what Detroit has accomplished in recent years, at least in a bricks-and-mortar way, happened without direct city money, from building Comerica Park and Ford Field (built with bonds floated by a local stadium authority) to real-estate deals like renovating the Book Cadillac Hotel and opening three casinos. It all happened without burdening the city's books. And it's hard to imagine that any of it could have developed if it had been up to the municipal government—broke, dysfunctional—to do it. "We're not looking for investments that reinforce existing patterns of behavior," Laura Trudeau, senior program director of the Troy-based Kresge Foundation, told me in a 2010

Architectural renderings depict the new Cobo Center riverfront facade and interior lobby scheduled to open by 2013. (Courtesy of Cobo Regional Conventional Facility Authority)

The dramatic improvements in Cobo occurred soon after the City of Detroit surrendered control of the asset to the regionally based nonprofit Cobo Regional Convention Facility Authority. (Courtesy of Cobo Regional Conventional Facility Authority)

interview. "We really want to try to help the city and the leaders of the city think differently about the future."

It recalls to my mind a remark that a German urban planner named Wennemar de Weldige made to me in Leipzig on a frosty December evening in late 2010. He was explaining to me how the city encouraged redevelopment of vacant industrial spaces like the one we were visiting, a former textile factory now filled with artists studios and galleries. The city mostly got out of the way of the entrepreneurs. "We can't give them money," he told me. "We can give only freedom."

If it's clear that I'm a fan of these "upstream" and "downstream" arrangements, I acknowledge that special-purpose entities like authorities and conservancies contain as many flaws as any human enterprise. They're not very democratic, for one thing; the public does not elect either their executives or the boards that choose those executives; board meetings take place outside the glare of publicity so common to other public-body deliberations; leadership usually rests in the hands of a few well-intentioned professionals, technocrats really, who may report to elected leaders now and then but otherwise are mostly left alone to do their jobs. Since foundations and other donors pay for most of the work of renovation and operations, perhaps the public shouldn't enjoy the right to object about how foundation dollars are being spent. But certainly key chunks of public property are being delegated to decision makers who operate mostly outside the scope of public review.

This independence sometimes creates real problems, and Robert Caro's Pulitzer Prize–winning biography of Robert Moses, *The Power Broker*, tells the tale of how master builder Moses seized the possibilities inherent in New York State's public authority law in the 1930s (a law brilliantly rewritten by himself) to amass enormous power for himself to reshape the city for good or ill. Indeed, some writers portray public authorities (of which there are thousands across the country, many dealing with public infrastructure and transportation systems) as a sort of shadow government—unelected, answerable to no one, often bent on bureaucratic empire building more than serving the public.

Then, too, these limited-purpose entities operate as such—with a limited purpose, whether it's to operate a riverfront promenade or a public market or a district like University Circle in Cleveland. No direct benefit derives to other parts of a city from one of these bodies, except in the general sense that an amenity anywhere helps the whole. No matter how many public authorities build however many stadiums or markets or river walks, city neighborhoods remain mostly untouched. In Detroit, the Riverfront Conservancy works marvels along the waterfront promenade, but just a few blocks inland the blight goes unabated.

So special-purpose entities by no means offer a cure-all answer. But because Detroit and other cities have gained so much with these bodies, it seems to me that devolving municipal powers downstream (or upstream to regional entities) makes all the sense in the world. One day the nonprofit group Midtown Detroit Inc., already doing real-estate developments and urban planning, could add even more capacity and grow into something like University Circle Inc. Detroit nonprofits like the Southwest Detroit Business Association and Warren-Conner Development Coalition already develop real estate and map urban planning strategies for the future; perhaps they, too, could take on UCI-like powers. And as Chris Ronayne of UCI says, his group, already policing its district and tending to public parks, may one day take on even more public powers handed off to them by a municipal government too broke and politically straitjacketed to do the work itself.

So far in this part of this book, we've looked at ways to reimagine city government from the outside. Sometimes, the work of re-engineering takes place *within* local government. We'll look at a prime example next.

THE LAND BANK MODEL

It's amazing how little we Americans know of the inner workings of our government. I'm referring not to backroom dealing over legislation—the "laws and sausages" that Bismarck cautioned us against watching. I'm talking about the everyday routine of issuing permits and flowing tax revenues through various funds and doing all the other minutiae that government does in our names. In my experience, even many elected officials know little about how their departments or agencies actually work day in and day out. There's always a second or third in command who's the operations guy (or woman), someone who's been there forever who keeps the place humming while the boss takes the bows.

It's rare that a public official understands the inner workings well enough to change them for the better. And even more rare is the public official who so masters the apparatus that he can play it like a flute, breathing new life into old systems.

One such rare individual is Dan Kildee, the long-time (1997–2009) treasurer of Genesee County, Michigan, the mid-Michigan area that encompasses the city of Flint. Maybe the sociologists who promote the 10,000-Hour Rule are right (the notion that one gets good at something only after practicing it for ten thousand hours). Certainly Kildee started his government career earlier than most, winning a seat on the Flint Board of Education at age eighteen. He then won a seat on the county's board of commissioners, serving there twelve years including five as chairman, before winning the county treasurer's post. (Kildee evidently has politics and government in his DNA; he's the nephew of longtime Flint-area congressman Dale Kildee.) So by the time he took over the job of collecting property taxes for Genesee County, he had already steeped himself in the intricacies of back-office government work.

And something struck him as odd.

Genesee County, like all counties in Michigan and in most other states, was taking ownership of a lot of property for unpaid property taxes. Most of those homes and stores and so on were in the county's poorer areas, especially in the city of Flint, the most economically depressed place in the county. And like virtually all counties, each year the Genesee County Treasurer sold off that inventory of tax-foreclosed property at an annual auction. Buyers could get the parcels for paying the back taxes; or, if nobody was willing to pay them, a buyer might pick up a parcel at a secondary sale later for as little as a few hundred dollars. Cities and counties had been taking title to tax-foreclosed properties and auctioning them off each year seemingly forever, a simple pass-through function.

Kildee's first insight, and perhaps the key to the whole thing, was that selling off tax-foreclosed parcels at auction did a lot more harm than good. Often the buyers were speculators operating from afar—infomercial watchers, Kildee calls them, people buying and selling from their laptops hoping to flip a parcel quickly for a profit, and abandoning it if they couldn't find a buyer. That, of course, meant that many a parcel came right back into the tax-foreclosure system— often several times in a row. The system all but guaranteed that once a property in a distressed area went vacant, it would likely stay vacant for a long time, perhaps permanently.

"There's just too much real estate in these places for the market to adequately absorb," Kildee says. "But in many of these cities, we continue to push property through these tax systems into these speculative sales as if somehow that market will just somehow catch on and begin to put these properties into productive use."

He continued, "It's completely irrational to think in a city that has surplus real estate, particularly surplus housing, that we can push more of it out there through these speculative auction sales through tax foreclosure. I don't know, maybe I'm missing something, but it just doesn't seem like it's going to work."

Nor did helping speculators feast on the bones of other folks' distress seem to reflect what government—the protector of the citizens' rights—ought to be doing. As Kildee asks, what are we thinking when we assume that the value to the community of a house or parcel of land is measured by how much money the county tax collector can get for it at public auction? Since when has the value of a place, of a neighborhood, of a family life, of the very place that we live our lives, been measured in dollars and cents?

"The fact that this property, to the local government, to the system that *we own*, was seen as only having its value determined by what we can sell it for to most speculative interests, I think is an indication how out of sync our systems are with our own true values," he says.

But how to change it? Kildee talked to Frank Alexander, a law professor at Emory University and a leading thinker on urban land issues, along with other experts, and together they all came up with a new approach. They took all the supposedly "worthless" tax-foreclosed land in abandoned neighborhoods in Flint and put it into the same pot as more valuable tax-foreclosed properties in the suburbs. Suburban residents could fall behind on their property taxes, too, but their properties generally fetched a lot more on the open market than did vacant lots and burned-out houses in Flint. Some parcels in this new pot might prove valuable and some might appear valueless, but the inventory *as a whole* showed immense promise, a rich stock of the only asset that we can never make more of—land.

As it happened, Michigan had recently changed its law on tax foreclosure so that parcels seized for delinquent taxes now went to the control of the county treasurer, not to the local city like Flint or Detroit. So Kildee, as Genesee County Treasurer, soon found himself in possession of a lot of parcels. He used the powers he and others found under existing Michigan law to create the legal authority known as the Genesee County Land Bank, and he conveyed all the county-owned, tax-foreclosed properties to this new authority. And he himself became chairman of the land bank.

Having formed the land bank, Kildee began selling off some of its parcels—mostly the more valuable ones in the suburbs—not at auction, and not to speculators and tax scavengers. Instead, the land bank listed those properties with Realtors who sold them in the conventional way, one at a time, for a price more in line with their market value. Before long, the land bank had cash coming in. And Kildee took that cash and turned around and used it to tend to the supposedly worthless parcels in Flint itself. The land bank demolished houses in Flint that were beyond repair or blighting an otherwise good neighborhood, and it paid for repairs to many others. Within its first five years, the land bank had demolished about a thousand eyesore houses in Flint and renovated about three hundred other properties, using the cash it raised from the sale of better parcels in its inventory.

Kildee also sparked a downtown revival by using land bank cash to fix up a vacant structure and moving the land bank's offices into the renovated space. Soon other downtown owners were upgrading their buildings, too. In a key project, the land bank provided incentives to developers to renovate the long-dormant Durant Hotel, located on a prominent overlook in downtown Flint. The eight-story, 250-room hotel was built in the 1920s; the land bank incentives have helped turn it into new residential units after it had been closed and shuttered for decades.

Kildee managed to wring yet more value out of the tax-foreclosed property. First, he saw that a lot of people pay their property taxes in full but pay them late, incurring hefty interest penalties. Since counties and other local units of government want their cash on time, many counties sell tax liens to investors—

Flint's Durant Hotel, long vacant and a symbol of the city's decline, underwent a dramatic renovation with the help of the Genesee County Land Bank. (Courtesy of Karp + Associates)

Flint's Durant Hotel. (Courtesy of Karp + Associates)

Flint's Durant
Hotel. (Courtesy of
Karp + Associates)

Flint's Durant
Hotel. (Courtesy of
Karp + Associates)

in effect, selling to tax scavengers the right to collect the unpaid tax, plus interest penalties that could run well above ten percent, in return for which these investors pay the county the amount of the delinquent taxes. Kildee asked himself, why not cut out the middleman? Why enrich those private investors with lucrative interest penalties that by law belong to the county? So he began borrowing the money not from tax-lien investors but from the bond market, selling "delinquent tax anticipation notes" at very low interest rates. He used that money to pay local municipal governments their share of tax revenue. And he retired the notes as he collected the delinquent taxes—keeping the hefty interest penalties for the county. It became a sweet form of arbitrage—borrowing at the very low rates available to counties and collecting at very high rates of interest. That alone pumped $1.6 million to $2.1 million a year into county coffers, to be used to rehabilitate and redevelop tax-foreclosed properties. And it happened all because Kildee understood the inner workings of the system and was willing to reinvent it.

Kildee's version wasn't the nation's first land bank authority. St. Louis had started the nation's first land bank as far back as 1971. Cleveland followed in 1976, Louisville in 1989, and Atlanta in 1991. But it was Kildee's creation of the Genesee County Land Bank in 2002 that introduced the very model of what a land bank should be. Kildee left his treasurer's post in 2009 to found the nonprofit Center for Community Progress to help cities elsewhere cope with their vacant land problems and set up land banks. By 2011, there were perhaps eighty land banks operating in cities and counties around the nation, and Kildee told me in mid-2011 that at the rate the concept was catching on, there might be twice that number in several more years.

To those who questioned the land bank's success, Michigan State University researchers reported that the land bank had raised property values throughout Genesee County by more than one hundred million dollars. And in 2007 the Kennedy School of Government at Harvard University named Kildee's Genesee County Land Bank the winner of its annual Fannie Mae Foundation Innovations Award for the best new idea in urban redevelopment.

When state lawmakers in Lansing, Michigan, revised the tax-foreclosure law again, Kildee did some more tinkering, helping rewrite the land bank authorization. The new law included a provision that any property owned by a land bank, which meant potentially any tax-foreclosed property, was by definition a brownfield—thus making all of a land bank's parcels eligible for brownfield tax credits. And, perhaps most important, the legal changes now allowed a land bank to seek a clear title to its parcels by authorizing a judge to do a mass action—in effect, to declare that a land title was "clean" with no prior holders having any further rights to it. That ability to scrub titles clean in a mass action proved a massive step. The often-interminable process of clearing title to abandoned properties in a city like Flint had now been compressed to a mere few months.

So the land-bank model, done properly, has become a powerful tool in taking control of vacant and abandoned land inside our distressed cities. As anyone who observes cities today can testify, we pay a high cost for losing control of this land. Kildee estimates that a vacant house costs a city much more in services than a home occupied by a family. A vacant house is much more likely to burn or host a crime. He estimates that every one percent increase in abandonment is matched by a more than double that increase in crime.

As Kildee says, we need to stop thinking of vacant and abandoned property as a nuisance, something to regulate and enforce and police and then simply liquidate. "We've got to recast our thinking so that we begin to think of land as real estate," he says, "as something that has value, that is worth something. If we treat it as if it's valuable, the market, that wonderful invisible hand, might accept that land as an asset. If you treat it as something to be sold at an auction for a bargain-basement price, that market will respond accordingly."

Of course, revamping the system this way doesn't endear land banks to the speculators and tax scavengers. "There are real interests in this country that benefit from the system the way it's devised right now," Kildee says.

That's where the irrationality comes into play. Consider what happens in Wayne County, the county that encompasses Detroit. As in most other counties, the Wayne County Treasurer's Office each year auctions off all the tax-foreclosed properties that have fallen to its care. At the height of the real estate boom in the mid-2000s, it auctioned about two thousand parcels a year in Wayne County, the majority of which were in Detroit itself. But as the real-estate bubble collapsed and foreclosures devastated Detroit, the number of tax-foreclosed properties sold at auction soared to fifteen thousand in 2011. Many if not most of those were vacant lots in Detroit, many no doubt going through foreclosure not for the first time, and everyone knew that land speculators were using the auction to feast on the bones of the city, buying land not for genuine redevelopment but simply hoping to flip the parcels for a quick profit, making no improvements and often paying no taxes. Yet the auction ground on, year after year.

Bringing about reform would mean first getting public officials and civic leaders to acknowledge what's going on. That may mean sending many of our leaders back to school to learn the mechanics of land policy even in their own communities.

"In our righteousness, in our indignation over what has happened over the last three or four years in the mortgage and housing crisis, let's not forget that we've got some homework to do ourselves, in the pubic sector, in fixing a system that mirrors the very same principles that we are so critical of," Kildee says. "And often our unwillingness to fix this system isn't because it's aligned with our values. It's because we don't even know this system exists. It sits behind the wall in the back shop of government."

Kildee's Genesee County model had not been underway long when fans of it in Detroit began to lobby Detroit's leaders to create their own land bank. It proved to be a frustrating, even exasperating, slog through the bureaucracy and intransigence of city leaders, especially at Detroit's City Council.

After years of frustrating the hopes of land-bank enthusiasts, the council finally approved the creation of a Detroit land bank in August 2008. It took the rest of that year and all of 2009 and into 2010 to organize the board of directors, interview candidates to run it, and otherwise get going. Aundra Wallace, a former senior vice president with the North Carolina Community Development Initiative, took over as director in April 2010. "It was an opportunity I thought to start an organization," Wallace told me later. "I thought that if you could get the right components together that you could really do some good things."

Wallace was shrewd enough to know that he lacked the sweeping powers conferred on Kildee's land bank in Flint. Detroit City Council may have relented by creating the land bank, but they skimped on its authority: Council conveyed none of the city's vast holdings of tax-foreclosed properties to the new land bank; gave it no direct city money; required that it buy any city-owned properties at fair-market value; and otherwise wished it luck and off you go.

"You've got to manage expectations," Wallace told me, sounding a theme he would return to again and again. "Detroit has had a decline in population for more than thirty years. So if you think you're going to be a savior as an entity, that's unrealistic."

"It's a grind. You're not going to get a lot of 'thank yous,'" he continued. "People are going to feel as if you're not doing enough. And you can't do enough because you don't have enough resources to do everything that needs to be done, whether the resources are human capital or financial capital. You just don't have all the resources to do it, and that's why you need to be strategic."

Despite the restrictions, the Detroit Land Bank Authority did attract some good working capital. The Ford Foundation was its first investor, giving one million dollars of seed money. The State of Michigan's Land Bank Authority followed with $12.3 million from their portion of federal Neighborhood Stabilization Program (NSP) money; and there were additional grants from Kresge Foundation, the Local Initiatives Support Corporation (LISC), a nonprofit that trains and funds neighborhood-level activism, and from the city's share of federal NSP money. All together, Wallace and his small but growing team (still fewer than a dozen staffers in all by late 2011) had some twenty million dollars to start making strategic investments. They bought seventy-five houses in target neighborhoods, mostly from commercial banks from their inventory of foreclosed houses (the REO sales), and then started paying crews to rehab them. The land bank acquired more property nearby their small housing stock through the Wayne County Treasurer's annual auction of properties seized through tax foreclosure, the idea being to protect the homes they were working on from blight nearby.

Wallace concentrated this first round of rehabbing in Detroit's East English Village and Morningside districts, areas with a growing problem of vacancy but still enough vibrancy to make them worth fighting for. Selecting the homes to buy became an art form. Detroit has a lot of great old mansions in districts like Boston Edison, houses that offer beautiful architecture but that can gobble energy in winter; they also tend to cost a good percentage of one's paycheck to renovate. Since the land bank was hoping to resell to working- to middle-class families, Wallace aimed his efforts at more manageable-sized houses.

That also meant assessing the surrounding neighborhood, not just a single available house. Wallace didn't intend to pour his money down a hole; if a neighborhood was sliding toward ruin, he would put his limited funds somewhere else.

"Since the funding that we have is so limited, we have to make sure we have the most impact that we possibly can when we acquire a house," he told me. "You have to manage everyone's expectations. I can't do everything. I'll have to be honest about that. And I'm not going to make everybody happy."

Speaking with Wallace, I may have let some of my enthusiasm for Kildee's model in Genesee County show through. We started talking about how the Genesee County Land Bank accepts all the tax-foreclosed properties in and around Flint, with powers to build, demolish, sell, or hold. The equivalent of that much inventory in Detroit, Wallace pointed out, would be something like sixty thousand abandoned parcels, mostly vacant lots that the City of Detroit owns. For those who want the Detroit Land Bank to emulate the Flint model, Wallace explained the facts of life:

> If all those properties came to the Detroit Land Bank Authority, it would sink the organization. Let me tell you why. We're the only land bank in the state of Michigan at the local level that does not have a direct affiliation with its county treasurer's office. That's number one. We receive no general fund support at all. So if you transferred sixty thousand lots over to the Detroit Land Bank Authority, I've got to have insurance on each of those sixty thousand parcels, and I've got to have a property maintenance budget for each parcel. And as a young organization, it goes back to my comment on managing expectations; we don't have the financial resources to do all of those things at this point in time. I have to be realistic about what we can and cannot take on.

As of early 2012, the Detroit Land Bank was busy rehabbing its one hundred or so houses, and had begun to sell off the first of them. No doubt its actions will help stabilize a block here and a block there; but hopes of widespread change midwifed by a land bank with powers akin to the Genesee County model have been stillborn. Perhaps nothing more could be expected from an organization so hamstrung by its founding charter.

Even so, I'd like to see what the Flint folks could have done with twenty million dollars in seed money, or for that matter any of the other dozens of land banks setting up around the country. The Detroit Land Bank in execution turns out to look like so many other revitalization efforts in the city—a good idea resisted by the city's leaders at first, then implemented reluctantly, and never given the powers and support it takes to make a big difference.

Skeptics suggest that land banks have been oversold as a solution in places like Detroit. Robin Boyle, chairman of the urban planning department at Wayne State University, notes that Detroit has many de facto land banks operating—the city itself owns thousands of parcels, as do the county and the state, and the Detroit Public Schools, the quasi-public Detroit Economic Growth Corporation, and other public agencies own available land. The land-bank model may be an important tool with well-designed powers to deal specifically with the problem of vacancy. But perhaps even more useful would be a unifying vision and cooperative action between all the many agencies—city, county, and state—that own land inside cities like Detroit and Flint.

Then, too, Kildee hastens to add that land banks are just one tool. Cities need to sharpen all their tools, including code enforcement and tax collections, to even dent the problem of vacant land. Mostly, though, he suggests that cities need to think anew about how they operate, to see new possibilities in old ways of doing things:

> Those systems were pretty much designed for a different time and a different place for a different era, for a time when all cities were growing, and land was appreciating in value, when it was fairly easy for the market to simply absorb a property that becomes available. So you fast forward now to the twenty-first century and you see that those systems, those state policy systems that either enable or limit the ability of local government to effectively deal with these problems, often have to be changed in order to give you, at the local level, tools you need.

Before we leave our examination of how we can govern cities better, we need to look at one more way to improve the effectiveness of city government. In many ways, it may be the most politically charged topic of all.

A GREAT IDEA DETROIT HAS NEVER TRIED

Ever since cities began to lose their residents, jobs, and tax base to the suburbs, urban planners have been trying to figure out how to reverse the trend—if not actually to bring back all those folks who fled to suburbia, at least to spark enough interest in the city to generate new development. To that end, for decades government at all levels has been pouring redevelopment dollars into our older, suffering cities. By the 1990s, it had become commonplace to say that cities absorbed all that aid like Lake Michigan absorbs a passing shower. Millions of dollars—indeed, tens of millions—had been spent in places like Flint and Buffalo and Youngstown and Detroit with seemingly not much to show for it. That lack of improvement in the underlying poverty rates, or in the bleak physical aspect presented by so many cities despite decades of government programs, has puzzled America and led many pundits, especially those of the conservative political bent, to conclude that cities were hopeless, and that we may as well turn off the aid spigot altogether.

But all wasn't lost or wasted; and valuable lessons have been learned about what works and what doesn't. To paraphrase what President Barack Obama once said of wars, we shouldn't be against all government aid to cities, just dumb aid to cities. A lot of federal aid has been wasted over the years in the sense that it did not spark the hoped-for spin-off private investment. But the smartest cities did make their way through the maze; they produced results both surprising and repeatable elsewhere. And that's the focus of this section on neighborhood revitalization—what works, and what doesn't, and why.

To understand the problem, let's think of city neighborhoods fitting into three categories. The "upper" neighborhoods enjoy a stable housing market, a population of mostly middle- or even upper-middle-income earners, an above-average percentage of owner-occupied houses, and an absence of vacancy and blight. "Middle" neighborhoods rank a little lower on the scale; they still enjoy strong assets such as historic architecture or proximity to a popular city park, but they bear the burden of an increasing number of low-income residents, a smaller percentage of stable, owner-occupied homes, perhaps more indicators of poverty such as a lot of single-mother-headed households, and a small but perhaps growing problem with vacancy and blight—all signs that the district may be headed for a tipping point toward failure. "Lower" districts suffer all the urban ills—large-scale poverty, abandonment, and blight; numerous indicators of social ills; many foreclosures, and so forth. In the history of community development efforts, most government aid to cities has gone toward the upper and lower neighborhoods, not to the middle. The upper neighborhoods enjoy the clout, connections, skills, and other resources to win city money for their districts; this is especially true of downtown residential enclaves, waterfront districts, and the like. And the poorest neighborhoods, while they may lack any of those strengths, find themselves the beneficiary of numerous local, state, and federal poverty programs aimed at the neediest residents. The lower districts may also benefit from the presence of community development organizations (CDOs), nonprofit groups that, to a greater or lesser degree, have grown skilled at grant writing and other techniques of winning dollars for their districts. Middle neighborhoods, by contrast, lack the clout of the upper districts and the large population of the poorest residents that, by government formulas, get most of the redevelopment aid sent their way.

Yet the great insight that developed by the mid-to-late '90s held that middle districts offered the greatest opportunity to make a difference. The upper districts already enjoyed an active housing market and didn't need much help to draw in private investment; the lower districts never seemed to improve no matter how much aid money came their way. Indeed in many parts of Detroit, Flint, Youngstown, and other cities, those districts declined even further despite the aid. The solution to the puzzle lies in the ability of neighborhoods to attract private investment, either from outsiders or from their own residents. The poorest districts suffer so much abandonment and remain so far removed from any sort of active, healthy real-estate market, that government aid dollars never bring these districts up far enough to a positive tipping point. And that tipping point is defined as a level sufficiently flush to entice outside investors, or to convince current residents that spending their limited cash on home repairs would bring them a return in higher property values.

Despite this insight, government aid dollars, including federal cash from Community Development Block Grant and the HOME housing improvement program, two federal programs that funnel money for redevelopment into cities, continued over the years to be spent on the lowest-income neighborhoods. Why? In part because policy rules restricted the spending of that money to the neediest citizens. And partly because even when politicians had more discretion, they tended to believe that limited resources should go toward those in greatest need. That was particularly true of the career staffers in many city departments; they brought to their work a culture of activism and belief in government's role in evening out society's inequalities. So even as many academics and urban planners and some politicians were beginning to suggest a more aggressive targeting of aid dollars to where they would do the most good—to those middle neighborhoods where a little money went a long way— most of the cash got spent elsewhere.

To cite one federal program: The Empowerment Zone endeavor of President Clinton's administration showered a hundred million dollars on Detroit, and newspaper writers and others dreamed of seeing real bricks-and-mortar change in the city's neighborhoods. But regulations restricted the cash to going to the neediest districts, where it was spent on social programs that, while no doubt worthwhile and supportive of the city's poorer residents, left no lasting trace. Indeed, Detroit's Empowerment Zone district today is emptier and poorer than before the money arrived.

By the late 1990s, cities were eager to try a new way.

RICHMOND'S NEIGHBORHOODS IN BLOOM

Case in point: Richmond, VA, and its acclaimed Neighborhoods in Bloom program. Begun in 1999, Richmond's NiB program offered one of the nation's most striking examples of a city targeting resources to a tiny number of distinct neighborhoods to make a real difference and spark renewed private investment. For five years, the program seemed to do everything right and provided an example for other cities to follow.

A little background: Richmond, the capital of the Confederacy, recovered from the pounding that General Grant's army gave it to become a southern industrial center by the early twentieth century. After World War II, it saw the same population drain to suburbia as everywhere else. By the 2000 census, its population had settled at just under two hundred thousand residents, many of them poor. The city government, like others elsewhere, garnered a lot of federal grant money to alleviate poverty under programs such as Community Development Block Grants and HOME. In 1998, the city administration

acknowledged that twenty-five years of sprinkling the anti-poverty funds
across broad areas of the city had failed to do much good. Individual blocks
and houses might be improved, but no neighborhoods had revitalized, and
the city could never declare victory and move on to the next area in need.
At the same time, the city's nonprofit neighborhood groups, the community
development organizations, or CDOs, complained that the city's annual process
of applying anew for CDBG and HOME dollars to support their work frustrated
their purposes. Since many CDOs worked on housing projects that took years to
achieve, they needed a longer-term, more stable commitment of dollars.

Faced with these issues, Richmond's acting city manager and others in city
government decided to concentrate grant resources on a handful of districts
to see if it would make a difference. How they chose which neighborhoods
provided a remarkable example of coalition building and data-driven decision-
making. Of forty potential target neighborhoods, six were chosen for NiB
targeting—Church Hill Central, Southern Barton Heights, Highland Park–
Southern Tip, Carver/Newtowne West, Blackwell, and Jackson Ward. A seventh
neighborhood, Oregon Hill, was later added to receive some targeted funds
but not other NiB services. The districts chosen showed strong needs—they
had poverty rates of at least thirty percent and often higher; vacant buildings
scarred the districts; often crime and other social ills flourished; single-mother
households dominated in some areas; expressways had slashed through some of
the districts, creating wounds from which neighborhoods had never recovered;
renter-occupied residences outnumbered owner-occupied residences; some of
the neighborhoods contained failed public housing projects.

At the same time, though, the districts offered appealing reasons for NiB
targeting. They were all clustered not far from downtown Richmond, offering
good views and a convenient location. They sported significant architectural
assets, with historic homes in the Federal, Greek Revival, Queen Anne,
Italianate, and other styles—many in need of repair, but providing good bones
for any future effort.

Richmond put NiB into operation in mid-1999. A real effort to include
neighborhood residents in the planning stood out from other less inclusive
efforts in other cities. In each NiB target area, the city created a team that

included neighborhood residents and civic organizations active in the area. Each team had a real say in mapping the precise areas to receive funds and developing work plans and budgets, down to specific buildings to be rehabilitated or demolished. Teams met monthly or bimonthly to keep it all on track.

And dollars poured into the NiB target areas. During the two years prior to NiB, the city had spent about $95,000 of its CDBG grant money in the target areas; over the five years of NiB, the city spent $6.1 million of CDBG money there. For the HOME program, the amount spent previously was just $15,000; under NiB, the amount was $4.5 million. At the same time, the Richmond office of the nonprofit Local Initiatives Support Corporation focused its subsidies for moderate-income housing programs on the NiB target areas, including grants, loans, and lines of credit. All this money paid for a lot of acquisition of blighted property, demolition, rehabilitation, and construction of new homes.

At the same time, the city focused extra staff time and resources in the NiB target neighborhoods. The city stepped up code enforcement; owners of dilapidated buildings got warning letters but also assistance to fix the blight. The city added staff to its law department and real-estate office to move vacant, tax-delinquent properties more quickly through the tax-foreclosure process. The historic designation review process sped up, from a typical six-month timetable to as little as two months. Residents who needed counseling about their housing needs got it, like seniors enrolled in the city's senior-citizen tax abatement program. In a few cases, the city provided relocation assistance to people displaced by the demolition and rehabilitation work.

The results were etched in dollars and cents. A 2006 review by three scholars—George Galster of Wayne State University in Detroit, John Accordino of Virginia Commonwealth University in Richmond, and Peter Tatian of the Washington, D.C.–based Urban Institute—deployed a rigorous statistical analysis to screen out other factors that might have influenced the result. "Although average home sales prices increased at a healthy clip citywide after 1996, they increased 9.9 percent per year faster in the target neighborhoods after the onset of the NiB program than they did elsewhere in the city," they wrote. In fiscal year 1990/91, home sales prices in the target areas averaged less than half of the citywide average. By fiscal year 2003/04, home sales prices in the target areas averaged seventy percent of the citywide price average.

And in a key finding, they said that when city investments in a given block exceeded a threshold of $20,100, the average home sale price increased by over fifty percent and continued to rise after that. That, if anything, demonstrated the point of the effort—that to do any good, to provide enough help to demonstrate to private investors that something good was happening in a sustained way— that the public dollars needed to focus laser-like on a neighborhood to bring redevelopment to a tipping point.

That investment threshold may be different for each city and each neighborhood, but there seems little doubt that a threshold exists. Galster, Accordino, and Tatian pointed out the need for a definition of neighborhood health precise enough to tell us how much to invest in a district and when to declare victory and move on. But their careful academic language cannot minimize the impact of their findings: "The results of this study lend support to the notion that the public and nonprofit sectors should target their resources so as to achieve a threshold level beyond which the private market can operate without subsidies (except where they are needed to maintain affordability or to preserve historic structures)."

And finally there is this: Richmond, which had lost population since 1950, actually gained residents in the years during and after Neighborhoods in Bloom was in place. The city saw its population rise 3.2 percent between 2000 and 2010, putting Richmond back above the two-hundred-thousand mark. We should hesitate to attribute the gain to any one program, or even to say that population gain or loss is the only yardstick that matters. An underlying principle of this book is the opposite, that cities can be great at any level of population. Nonetheless, the coincidence of targeted resources, rising property values, and people moving back in to the city remains intriguing.

A footnote: Even five years of successful efforts could not protect Neighborhoods in Bloom from the ravages of politics. Richmond had created NiB when it governed itself under a city-manager system. In 2003, voters in Richmond adopted an elected-mayor form of government, with former Virginia governor Doug Wilder overwhelmingly elected mayor the following year. Under Wilder, the emphasis shifted, and the strong partnership between city planners and neighborhood activists weakened. In mid-2005, Wilder announced the city would join a new program, the Vacant Properties Campaign, a multi-city effort to track and reclaim vacant and abandoned properties in the city. "This is a wonderful opportunity for the city and its residents," Wilder's chief administrative officer, William Harrell, said at the time. "Richmond has done tremendous work targeting problem properties with the Neighborhoods in Bloom program, but we must now turn our attention to the nearly 2,500 blighted buildings throughout the city."

In a way, the diminishment of NiB in Richmond, to be replaced by other well-meaning programs, cannot detract from the lessons learned: well-conceived, neighborhood-supported, data-driven targeting of limited resources works.

Exactly why does it work? Dale Thomson, a professor of political science at the University of Michigan Dearborn who has studied and written extensively about targeting, cites several possible reasons why the tactic produces results. Besides the actual impact of all that new cash, there are several reasons. First, there are the savings in transactional costs: redevelopment staffers concentrate their efforts in a few discrete environments, therefore saving time, money, and energy on a cost-per-unit basis to achieve economies of scale. Then there are multiplier effects that occur when concentrated dollars spark private investment that otherwise would have stayed away. Then, too, a well-publicized targeting campaign creates a heightened focus or awareness of a neighborhood's assets and its revitalization, which often brings in more investment. And often we see a spillover effect, as in Richmond, when adjacent districts not receiving targeted dollars nonetheless enjoy additional investment as part of the general upswing.

By the way, the variables used to select middle neighborhoods might vary from city to city or report to report, but generally they cover such indicators as vacancy rates, housing sales, percent of owner-occupied housing (recommended to be at fifty percent or higher to be considered good), the housing cost burden (the percentage of household income spent on housing; the citywide average was about thirty percent), and so forth. In the most elaborate targeting schemes, data analysts use these and many other variables to create scores for each neighborhood and, in places like Richmond, used these rankings as well as common sense to choose which middle markets to target.

DETROIT: DIFFERENT STORY

A lot of cities—Richmond, Baltimore, Cleveland, Battle Creek, Youngstown—have tried targeting to some greater or lesser degree. They were all post-industrial cities that have suffered many of the same ills as Detroit. Yet these cities found a way to target their limited resources to do some good, in a way that eluded Detroit during these same years. So the question arises: Why didn't Detroit embrace targeting of resources for greater impact as these other cities did?

Certainly people had been suggesting a targeting strategy in Detroit for some time. In 1999, a group of Wayne State University planning students proposed to Detroit's Planning and Development Department that it create a series of Neighborhood Stabilization Zones in middle neighborhoods and target aid dollars there. One of the students, Peter Zeiler, now director of transit-oriented development in Charlotte, NC, told me in 2011 that targeting middle neighborhoods was the only way to achieve any results, even though, as he acknowledged, the political infighting could be brutal; it would mean taking at least some dollars away from the neediest neighborhoods. The suggestion wasn't taken; nobody, he said, was willing to admit that putting dollars in the poorest, most abandoned districts, as Detroit had been doing for years, was doing little good. Zeiler likened the choice to that of flying over a forest fire misting a few droplets of water everywhere—and doing no good at all—versus taking a stand in one quadrant and pouring in resources. As he put it, "Either *some* neighborhoods go down, or *all* neighborhoods go down." Another nudge came in 2003, when the US Housing and Urban Development Department criticized Detroit's stewardship of federal aid for a lack of accountability and impact, and suggested a more aggressive targeting strategy. And in 2005, a group of planning students at the University of Michigan wrote a 157-page report titled "On Target: A Housing Strategy for Detroit," that laid out in precise, professional detail how the city could put its discretionary dollars to best use.

Yet the city hesitated. Sheila Cockrel, the longtime city council member now teaching at Wayne State University, suggests that the social-worker backgrounds of so many key Council leaders over the years played a role in shaping how the city distributes aid. Both Erma Henderson and Maryann Mahaffey, who collectively served as president of Detroit's city council for twenty years, rose to prominence through social work and civil rights advocacy. Sheila Cockrel suggests that this early training fostered a culture that prized the social safety net above all else; better that each of the most needy districts gets a little than a lucky few districts get a lot. Dale Thomson calls this the "politics of poverty"; it rewards, he says, "city officials for prioritizing policies that primarily benefit the city's large low-income population even when those policies may have a negative effect on the city's ability to attract investment and ensure financial sustainability." Layer in the combative union-management antagonism that marked Detroit's signature auto industry for decades—a predilection for confrontation and an attitude of entitlement that permeated all aspects of life in the metropolitan area—and we begin to see why civic leaders as a class in Detroit might distrust purely market-driven solutions no matter how data driven they are. The problem arises, of course, when giving everyone a dollop of aid proves more or less useless as a solution to urban ills.

Nor can we forget the corrosive influence of politics upon the choices Detroit leaders have made. We'll look at two cases, the so-called "targeting" practiced during then-mayor Kwame Kilpatrick's Next Detroit Neighborhood Initiative circa 2006 and the way Council has handed out cash over many years from the federal program known as Community Development Block Grants.

Our guide for the first will be Alan Levy, who early in Kilpatrick's first term (2002 and 2003) headed the city's Office of Neighborhood Commercial Revitalization. Levy, a professional planner who had worked in San Diego prior to coming to Detroit, knew some of the trends in planning were shifting toward using a data-driven approach to targeting resources; and one day he wrote a one-page summary suggesting a more data-driven approach using sensible criteria to decide where to invest resources. He showed it to his bosses within his department of city government—Planning and Development—and they responded enthusiastically, as did Kilpatrick himself when he saw it later. But it was still just a one-pager, and not much came of it then.

After Kilpatrick's reelection, though, in 2005, the idea floated to the top again, and Levy, by then deputy director of Planning and Development, joined many others from the administration on a team to select areas for the mayor's signature Next Detroit Neighborhood Initiative, the phrase "Next Detroit" being the prefix for a variety of Kilpatrick efforts then. They talked up targeting and retained the three *r*'s from Levy's original memo—reinforce, revitalize, redevelop—but from the beginning, the effort went off in a direction Levy remembers as distinctly odd. Not the least of the worries was that Kilpatrick had put the chief of staff in his office, Christine Beatty, in charge of the effort (the same Beatty, as the world later learned, who was Kilpatrick's secret lover and eventual fellow perjurer, a choice that earned both jail terms in a text-message scandal a couple of years later). And nobody on the team was really using data or strict criteria to drive the decision making.

"It was a little bit weird to me that this planning process was being driven by somebody out of the mayor's office who had no planning background," Levy said in 2011 of Beatty's role. "But even more importantly, Planning and Development was only one of maybe ten to twenty departments that had a voice in this process." The people from other departments all put in their suggestions for which neighborhoods to target, and naturally most chose places where they already were working as a way to reinforce their existing programs. As Dale Thomson writes, "Modest efforts to imbue the process with rationality were quelled quickly."

One deserving and promising neighborhood, Southwest Detroit, seemed to make a good choice. It enjoyed a network of community development organizations with years of success behind them, as well as a growing population of Latino immigrants that made it one of the handful of districts in the city to be gaining population. Yet Kilpatrick excluded it on the grounds that it was already working well and didn't need public investment. But, as Thomson says, "Even mayoral allies acknowledged that the area was excluded because it failed to support the mayor in the last election."

Some of the districts that did make the cut also raised concerns. Brightmoor was included—a district so distressed that, as Thomson says, a history of public and private redevelopment aid "had been continually overwhelmed by broader socioeconomic forces." Brightmoor did, however, offer votes. And then there was a northwest district known as Grand River/Greenfield, an area that didn't meet objective criteria for selection; it lacked a local community development organization for example. Yet a politically connected private developer and ally of the mayor did own several major commercial properties at the main intersection, and that was enough.

"It was obviously very political about what areas they were going to pick," Levy said. "It just got pretty obvious that the decision on what the neighborhoods were going to be was driven out of the mayor's office and everybody else was going to sign off on it." He added by way of understatement, "I was removed from that process. I was not expressing totally fidelity to the direction." He left the city later and now works as a private consultant.

Kilpatrick eventually announced six chosen neighborhoods, two that were said to be in very distressed shape, two in more moderate condition, and two that were doing pretty well. Interestingly, activists in other parts of the city did not raise too loud a protest over being left out. Partly, Thomson suggests, that was because Kilpatrick had promised to include other neighborhoods as the program continued; and partly because veteran activists doubted that NDNI would amount to very much and so "they felt no need to object," he says. And, if that was the expectation, it was correct. Money just trickled in, in part because the city's internal departments suffered what Abraham Lincoln once called "the slows," and partly because foundations were skeptical of dealing directly with the city and were already looking for other ways to make a difference. Besides, it wasn't long before Kilpatrick's attention was drawn into his losing battle to stay out of jail. Nothing much came of the NDNI effort.

Just as wasteful over the years has been Detroit's distribution of federal funds under the Community Development Block Grant program. CDBG gives city councils one of their few really discretionary pots of money to hand out. But if Cleveland and other cities targeted this resource, giving a smaller number of qualified nonprofits enough money to make a difference, Detroit's city council for years handed out dribs and drabs of cash to hundreds of recipients, including churches, local community development organizations, and the like. Often the money did little if any good. If a local organization needed, say, one hundred thousand dollars to complete a project, it might have to apply two or three years in a row (since the funds were allocated annually) to get enough to move the project along. And sometimes the money just went to keep a staffer on payroll. "Our philosophy in Detroit was always put the money where it's most needed as opposed to where it's most useful," Levy told me.

The problem is not unique to Detroit. Presley Gillespie, a former banker who now serves as director of the Youngstown Community Development Corporation in that Ohio city, told me during one of my visits that as a banker he had subsidized numerous scattered-site housing projects in the city with nothing to show for it except a few small projects that failed or limped by.

Dale Thomson, the professor from UM Dearborn, has studied the way limited resources get spread around Detroit: "We've been investing money for years and years and years, we've poured millions and millions of dollars, and what do we have to show for our results? Very little. . . . It's a culture of helping the worst off and targeting the neediest, and the politics of poverty we have at the city council level where you gain by arguing for the least fortunate and you lose by trying to impose some sort of rationality that suggests we're going to talk about markets as a good thing, make decisions based on markets, or deny organizations that have great passion but don't have capacity."

And George Galster, the Wayne State University professor who co-wrote the Federal Reserve report on Richmond's Neighborhoods in Bloom success, is even blunter:

> I think that Detroit has been a case study of how to waste CDBG money by not adequately targeting it to particular places for a sustained amount of time. They are apparently unwilling to pay a little political price to pick some winners. They want everyone to have a little piece of the pie, which means nobody ever reaches critical levels to get the private market re-engaged, and so nobody gets leverage on their investments and the money essentially is not multiplied at all by private money and doesn't have much of an impact anywhere.

In more recent years, the Council has somewhat reduced the number of groups getting CDBG grants, and there have been greater efforts to use rational criteria in handing out resources. But Thomson still finds much lacking: "There's no real one answer, but from my perspective it's mainly institutional in the city. There's no culture of targeting in the city. And there's no culture of making a decision and really committing to it and using that to drive your decision making for a long period of time rather than a six month window or something like that. And while there is growing support for targeting, there's not a real strong appreciation for the type of criteria you need to use to select target areas to have the optimal impact, and there's certainly not much appreciation for targeting middle neighborhoods."

As I write this in mid-2012, Detroit mayor Dave Bing's administration was drawing fire for its willingness to suggest shutting off city services to the most abandoned neighborhoods as a way to save money better directed elsewhere. That Bing and his staff would even raise the possibility shows, perhaps, that some of the lessons of targeting have been learned. Whether it's too little too late remains to be seen.

REIMAGINING GOVERNMENT

Detroit's civic leaders, like those in many other cities, have a habit of proclaiming bold policies but delivering actions that are mostly feeble and incremental. Any changes implemented tend to be tweaks of existing policies and programs. Politics and bureaucratic infighting tend to get the blame; mayors, department heads, city council members, and their staffs all want to keep their jobs and maintain their budgets. In such an atmosphere, true reinvention looks too dangerous. And so in municipal governments today we see almost none of the entrepreneurial zeal and relentless devotion to results that gave us, say, the iPhone and other marvels of our age.

But in operations like Cleveland's University Circle Inc., Detroit's Eastern Market, Richmond's Neighborhoods in Bloom, and Flint's land bank, we do see real invention at work. People like Chris Ronayne, Dan Kildee, the Eastern Market leadership team—these people have reimagined city government, mostly by seeing that underfunded, understaffed, and politically dysfunctional municipal corporations can no longer do what we invented them to do, and so need to be replaced, or at least supplemented by new structures. These new structures operate either "upstream" or "downstream" from city government—at the regional and state levels or at the neighborhood level, whatever works best.

Perhaps true reinvention would involve recognizing the regional nature of metropolitan life, and therefore sharing revenues and tax base between the poorer, older city and its more prosperous, newer suburbs. The Minneapolis-St. Paul area has been doing something like this for many years; its regional revenue-sharing system distributes a slice of property-tax revenue from new development region wide, not just within the tiny township where a project takes place. And of course the Sunbelt cities that we've mentioned, Phoenix and Houston and San Antonio and many others, manage that trick by annexing their suburbs to re-create a more balanced tax base for municipal governance.

But short of that metropolitan sharing, perhaps the most we can hope is to break off pieces of the municipal function and give them to people and groups that can handle them better than the strapped, inept city government. At the very least, we need to admit that the municipal model in America today is broken—broken beyond repair—and that no amount of tinkering can make it whole again. Basic reinvention must be the order of the day.

3

SCHOOLS, PLUS A WORD ABOUT CRIME

Not long after a young software entrepreneur named Peter Karmanos Jr. co-founded the Compuware company in 1973, he moved his family from Detroit to the suburbs. The prod was the day one of his sons came home from elementary school with an A in reading.

"I had been working with him in his reader every day, and he couldn't read," Karmanos told me many years later. He went to see the boy's teacher.

"'Mr. Karmanos; Nick's one of my best students,'" he recalled the teacher saying. "'He really wants to learn; he comes to school prepared.'"

The prospect of his kids getting *A*'s but not learning anything prompted Karmanos to move his family to suburban West Bloomfield. One afternoon not long after they moved, he got a call from his son's new teacher. "Mr. Karmanos, we've tested your son, Nick, and he doesn't have any learning disabilities but . . ."

"But he can't read," Karmanos interrupted.

"Not a lick," she said.

"That's why we're here," he told her. Then he told her his son got an *A* from his previous reading teacher.

"Where was that?" she asked. He told her Detroit Public Schools, and she said, "Oh, my God."

Of all the urban ills that drive families from cities like Detroit, inadequate public schools rank at or very near the top. Worries about schools explain why the only people who seem to move into Detroit today are either the young and childless or the empty nesters. It's commonplace to see young families stay in Detroit only until their children get to age four or five, whereupon they decamp for the suburbs and more highly rated school systems.

The problem of low-performing schools is not, of course, limited to Detroit, but it appears to be most acute there. At the end of 2011, the Detroit Public Schools' performance on a national academic test showed that the district continued to rank worst among large cities in reading and math. In fourth-grade math, only 34 percent of DPS students scored at or above the basic level, compared to 74 percent of students in large cities and 82 percent nationally. On the reading portion of the test, 31 percent of fourth-graders scored at or above basic level compared to 55 percent in large cities and 66 percent nationally. In eighth-grade math, 29 percent of DPS students scored at or above basic level, compared to 63 percent in large-city districts and 72 percent nationally. In eighth-grade reading, 43 percent of DPS students scored at or above basic, compared to 65 percent in large cities and 75 percent nationally. The district's fourth- and eighth-grade students were among children in 21 cities who took the rigorous National Assessment of Educational Progress tests. While Detroit showed slightly higher scores than in 2009, when the tests were previously taken, the gains were classified as "not significantly different," by the National Center for Education Statistics, which oversees the tests.

Faced with disappointing results in many big cities, Americans have engaged in a running debate in recent years about how to improve school performance. If you follow the debate from afar, you may think the answer is any one of the following bromides: charter schools, vouchers, school uniforms, standardized testing, eliminating teachers unions, smaller class sizes, home schooling, longer school days, longer school years, more money . . . more money . . . more money. Dig a little deeper, and you can make a pretty good case that none of these things matters, in the sense that not one of them will create good schools by itself, and some of them have little or no impact even in conjunction with other steps.

So what works? Teacher quality and school leadership are the most important predictors of school achievement. Or, to put it another way, what matters is what happens in the classroom. And we have done enough experimentation by now, documented enough successes and failures, benefitted from enough rigorous studies of low-income yet high-performing schools, to glean a pretty good idea of how to improve education in our cities.

If there were any American school district destined to lie forgotten in the vale of failure, it would be the public schools of Inkster, a tiny industrial nodule on the outskirts of Detroit. Inkster shares with Detroit all the deforming problems of the age. Up until a few years ago, its Baylor-Woodson Elementary was one of the low-income, low-performing schools so prevalent in cities today. Student test scores were abysmal. Poverty indices were high: some ninety-eight percent of students are African American, and more than four out of five qualified for free or reduced-priced meals. When Thomas Maridada, the superintendent who took over Inkster schools in 2005, first visited Baylor-Woodson, he saw what he calls "intellectual genocide" at work, the abandonment of yet another generation of poor inner-city children in an American city.

Visit Baylor-Woodson today, and witness a water-into-wine miracle. The vast majority of the students meet state reading and math standards, even the tougher standards imposed in 2012. Well over half the students score as advanced in math and reading. Enrollment soared in recent years as the educational achievement levels rose; as a school of choice, open to students from nearby districts, Baylor-Woodson now welcomes students from Detroit and several suburbs. The Education Trust, a nationwide nonprofit school-improvement effort, awarded Baylor-Woodson its national Dispelling the Myth Award for its high academic performance.

Everyone acknowledges that the gains began when Maridada showed up as district superintendent. Born in Brazil and the oldest of five children, Maridada's family moved to Detroit when he was a child. The family lived in the old Brewster-Douglass housing projects. There was a day years earlier when future stars like Diana Ross and Smokey Robinson emerged from those projects, but Maridada today recalls the place as gang ridden and ugly. Young Thomas hadn't learned to read English yet when a teacher told him he would never amount to anything because of his poor language skills. Heartbroken, he told his mother, who gave her son a stiff dose of encouragement and self-reliance. "'She doesn't get the opportunity to name you,'" Maridada recalls his mother saying. "'She doesn't get the opportunity to dictate what you're going to be, how far you're going to go, what your life's opportunities are going to be. Only you and God get the opportunity to decide how far you will go.'" And his mother gave him new ways to see himself: "'She has named you incompetent. She has named you unworthy. But I rename you genius. I rename you full of hope. I rename you full of possibilities. I rename you a winner. Now go out and live up to your name.'"

The success of Baylor-Woodson Elementary demonstrates what a drive for excellence, good leadership, and attention to the basics of classroom teaching can accomplish. (Author photo)

Baylor-Woodson Elementary. (Author photo)

It didn't matter in the Maridada apartment if teachers did not assign homework. Thomas's mother would take her children to the public library for books. "I thought that everyone in the projects when the street lights came on actually sat at their dining-room table and read Shakespeare and *I Know Why the Caged Bird Sings*," Maridada said in 2011. "One of the things that I learned growing up in the projects is that no one determines your excellence. You can be excellent in the belly of hell if that's what you choose to do."

He carried that determination with him when he became a teacher, later an assistant principal, then a principal, and in 2005 when he took over the Inkster district, a system so wracked with problems that the state had taken over the district's finances and the children were mostly failing.

"We are shaken by genocide that we see in the Sudan," Maridada said much later. "But we are not shaken by intellectual genocide where kids have no hope. There's no one to push them and to tell them that they can be great, they can be dynamic, they can be more."

So Maridada told the Inkster kids that. Maridada implemented tough new teacher tenure and evaluation reforms, better matching the appropriate teachers with the right students. He negotiated a new teacher contract to find cost savings in benefits, which allowed him to pay better salaries to attract stronger teachers. At Baylor-Woodson, the school helps make up student's deficiencies by providing hot meals, field trips, and academic enrichment. A mobile dental lab helps fix the kids' teeth, and local eye doctors donate glasses. In terms of instruction, Maridada introduced a system pioneered by Dr. Lorraine Monroe, a leadership consultant who was the founding principal of the Frederick Douglass Academy, a successful middle and high school in New York City's Harlem district. Monroe created a system known as the Blackboard Configuration. The BBC serves as a rigorous outline detailing specific steps for students during each day's instruction period. A typical BBC would include a "Do Now" or starter activity to introduce a topic, the learning objective, the day's agenda, and a homework assignment. Baylor-Woodson principal Beverly Gerhard told me it requires a lot of preparation by teachers, but the system keeps everybody on track and lets students know what's expected of them.

At the district-wide level, Maridada created special academies in Inkster's high school in four categories: performing arts, international business and entrepreneurship, pre-engineering and science, and allied health; students take their high school classes in the morning and attend nearby Wayne County Community College classes in the afternoon. Maridada sent students to shadow doctors at Johns Hopkins Hospital in Baltimore and to attend plays in New York. Clear new objectives for math and reading were posted on classroom walls. Maridada, along with Baylor-Woodson principal Gerhard and teachers at all the Inkster schools, collaborated to transform the culture to make it learning and achievement centered, including creating a Saturday academy.

Darryl Love, principal of Meek-Milton, another Inkster school, said the improvements all started with Maridada's relentless focus on student achievement. "He set the vision for rigorous instruction in the classrooms, professional development for teachers, to be a data-driven district," Love told me during my visit to the school. "Just believing that every kid can succeed and will succeed. When we have them here, it's our responsibility to give them the best education possible. Don't take any excuses."

Sometimes, Maridada recalled, teachers might say to him he didn't understand the horrific at-home problems that held students back—a father in prison, say, or a mother on crack. "And I say to them, 'What does that have to do with your excellence?'"

The results could be seen in the rapidly improving test scores, but the real payoff came in the students' lives. Not long after Maridada began the reforms, a student named Tawanna Hudson told an interviewer how much difference it had made at her school. "It was noisy, and the behavior problems were terrible," the eighteen-year-old Hudson said. "Now it's excellent. I wish I could stay more years." And Janice Lloyd, mother of a high school student named Janet, credited the special academies Maridada set up with inspiring her daughter. "My daughter was always an exceptional student and never studied, but this program made her start opening her books," she said. Daughter Janet became co-valedictorian of her class.

"When kids who have graduated come back and tell me they are graduating from college, that to me is the standard of how successful your kids are," Maridada said. "I am successful if they are able to join society and have opportunities."

Other districts in other cities have achieved many of the same results by following many of the same routes. In the Charlotte-Mecklenburg district in North Carolina, the number of schools failing to hit their improvement targets shrunk to nine in 2010 from sixty-four in 2006. The graduation rate rose to 70 percent in 2010 from 66.4 percent a year earlier. How'd they do it? Through a relentless commitment to getting good teachers in the classrooms. Charlotte is now home to the Charlotte Teachers Institute, modeled after the Yale Teachers Institute, a program that during summer breaks gives teachers intensive content training to make them more knowledgeable about their subjects. The district also participates in the Teach For America program, supported by a gift of four million dollars from a Charlotte civic leader, assigning these enthusiastic teaching recruits to troubled schools for two-year stints; more than a third of them—thirty-eight percent in a two-year period—chose to stay in the district after their initial two-year assignment.

Meanwhile, the district created a strategic staffing project to get high-performing leaders and teachers into some of the district's most troubled schools. Under this program, the district offered financial incentives to good principals and teachers; once assigned to a problem school, a new principal could bring an assistant principal, an academic facilitator, and as many as five teachers with them. (Principals could also remove up to five staff members who were underperforming; they would be put on improvement plans, or, in some cases, dismissed.) A more rigorous data-driven analysis of student achievement accompanied each new team at a school. The district introduced strategic staffing in 2008, and the early results have been promising. Academic performance, as measured by proficiency on state tests, rose at nearly every school, and at some schools it jumped more than twenty points in just one year. Encouraged, the district, which started the program with seven schools in 2008, has been adding more than a dozen more.

This emphasis on high-quality teachers in classrooms has become the motif in many school reform efforts, said Amber Arellano, executive director of the nonprofit Education Trust-Midwest. In a 2012 interview, she told me, "There's this huge body of research around how absolutely fundamental it is to have a really high-performing teacher in high-poverty classrooms."

"Success is intentional," Nelson Henry, program director at Baylor-Woodson, added. "It is not accidental. The number-one indicator for success for a student is the teacher-student relationship. If you have dynamic teachers in front of students, they will learn."

The emphasis on good teachers, student achievement, and settling for nothing less than excellence by now motivates a great many efforts in a great many cities. The relatively new Excellent Schools Detroit, a nonprofit effort that encourages and popularizes school-improvement strategies, has set a goal of placing every Detroit student in an excellent school by 2020. Dan Varner, the head of the effort, defines an excellent school as one where ninety percent of kids graduate on time, ninety percent of elementary graduates go to a quality secondary school, and ninety percent of them are ready to succeed without remediation.

Varner told me that excellence in education imposes tough demands on parents. "There are a lot of families in this region that don't have any children's books at home for their youngsters. . . . When children show up at kindergarten and they don't have basic literacy and numeracy skills, they can't count to ten, they don't recognize the letters of the alphabet, they're behind already. And to play a catch-up game the entirety of those twelve years, that's hard work."

But excellence also requires parents to be savvy shoppers for education. Public schools are no longer a commodity, Varner told me.

"The day is gone that you and I grew up in where you defaulted to your neighborhood school. There are still a lot of folks who just do that, and that's not the way to do the greatest service to your kids. To do the greatest service to your kids, you've got to shop for education now. You've really got to go about choosing a school instead of defaulting to one."

We're just now getting to a good understanding of what creates high-achieving schools in low-income areas. Despite decades of talking about reform, true turnarounds of the type accomplished in Inkster and Charlotte-Mecklenburg began only a decade or less ago. But even with that short track record, we can safely make the following observations:

Be agnostic about governance. A great school can operate under a public school system or as a charter, private, or parochial school. Indeed, data provided by the Education Trust-Midwest on test results in Detroit schools show that regular public schools and charters were spread about evenly through the distribution of results. Charters in general have not moved the needle all that much on educational reform because most re-create the same conditions that exist in the adjacent public schools—the same grade structure, the same curriculum, in some cases even the same teachers and principals who have just moved over. The schools highlighted in this section—Baylor-Woodson Elementary and the Charlotte-Mecklenburg district—are both public school systems. Great schools can be found in any type of system.

Nor does the presence or absence of a teachers union make the difference. There are high-achieving schools where unions represent teachers and low-performing schools without teacher unions, and vice versa. At Baylor-Woodson, Nelson Henry not only headed the instructional programs when I visited, but he served for a time as president of the local teachers union. Either system can work, he told me, as long as teachers commit themselves to best practices including new data-driven measurements of achievement. Admittedly, in some districts a teachers union may be guilty of obstructing the introduction of new teacher evaluations and other reforms. If that detracts from focusing on the kids, then that has to change. "We have to teach students. We can't hide behind the contract," Henry said.

And we need to explore new forms of governance for schools, Dan Varner of Excellent Schools Detroit told me. "We default right now to a locally elected school board as a matter of state law," he said. Cities and parents "should be allowed to choose from a laundry list of options—elected school board, mayoral-run schools, Council-appointed school board, appointed or elected superintendent." In a spirit of vivid experimentation, he even suggests we stop promoting children by age, with all the nine-year-olds in one grade and the ten-year-olds in the next, and so forth. Why not, he asks, promote strictly by achievement level, with the brightest kids moving up faster?

Perhaps the best single indicator of the type of school we need to see was the reaction at Baylor-Woodson in early 2012 to the most recent tests scores from Michigan's standardized Michigan Educational Assessment Program (MEAP) tests. Baylor-Woodson students had been scoring near the top of the charts in previous years, notching achievement levels above ninety percent in some cases (meaning that percentage of students were performing at their grade level). In the early 2012 results, the test measurements were stiffened to give a better indication of student achievement, and Baylor-Woodson scores settled a little lower—down all the way to about the eighty-percent level in most cases. School officials in numerous districts would celebrate scores at the eighty-percent level, but Inkster district superintendent Mischa Bashir seemed genuinely troubled when I asked her about it. She and Principal Gerhard and the teachers at Baylor-Woodson would use the scores to detect weak spots, she told me, adding, "It's an opportunity for us to work harder and smarter."

Great teaching is a team effort. In years past (certainly when I was in elementary school) a teacher faced students alone for much of the day, and indeed for much of the school year. The principal loomed as a distant authority figure, best avoided.

"Oftentimes teachers lock their door, and they're not comfortable with administrative supervisors coming in," Inkster superintendent Bashir told me. But at Baylor-Woodson, visits by the principal, the head of instruction, and other collaborators have become part of the culture. The concept extends beyond the classroom. At Baylor-Woodson, teachers meet for a common forty-five-minute planning session every school day (the students go to various activities for that time). The teachers collaborate on lesson plans, talk over the latest data on student achievement, go over strategies to teach writing or math or science. As head of instruction, Nelson Henry would meet at least weekly with each teacher. "We have that sense of collaboration," he said. "We exchange ideas, maybe do some lesson planning together, so it's definitely a cohesive effort."

In a telling phrase, Bashir added, "We like to think that we have de-privatized teaching."

Data is critical. Testing has always been key to benchmarking success in schools, but now higher-performing schools and districts are paying ever more attention to results. In a weak environment, that may mean nothing more than "teaching to the test" at the expense of broader educational goals. But at places like Baylor-Woodson, it means using test data to spot the weak points and areas that need improvement, and thus guiding future efforts.

Excellent Schools Detroit, the nonprofit agency, has developed its own report cards on local schools, the rankings based on student test scores, teacher and student surveys, and site visits at which teams of volunteers arrived unannounced to examine a school for all manner of things, including safety, cleanliness, and the quality of the interaction between students and teachers. These visits are not scheduled in advance, but the schools all have opted into the program and know that a team visit will come within a given time. As of early 2012, all Detroit Public Schools and dozens of charters had opted in to the program.

In the Charlotte-Mecklenburg district, the district has participated in the Measuring Effective Teaching study, funded by the Bill & Melinda Gates Foundation. The study has been examining the practices of thousands of teachers in six districts across the country, including nearly 500 teachers in the Charlotte-Mecklenburg schools. The results are expected to help guide districts in defining what constitutes good teaching and in training effective teachers for the future.

After some years serving Inkster public schools and being named Michigan Superintendent of the Year in 2008, Thomas Maridada moved on to the Pontiac School District north of Detroit, where he continued to insist on excellence in the face of poverty and failure. He created a college partnership with nearby Rochester College, Oakland Community College, Oakland University, and Baker College, in which select Pontiac High School students take regular courses alongside college students. He also started more of the special academies in science, math, and other subjects at various elementary schools. In 2011, Maridada accepted a new role in education policy in Washington, DC.

In a speech at Rochester College in 2011, Maridada recounted something he had seen once in a nature program on television. Water buffalo were crossing a stream when alligators set upon the youngest. The remainder of the water buffalos turned back and relentlessly drove away the predators, saving their youngest.

"That is our analogy for life," Maridada told his listeners. "You have a responsibility to be just like the pack of water buffalos who did not allow that baby who had a certain fate of death to be destroyed. You have a responsibility to go back and save somebody."

And he added, "One person can make a difference, but oh my God, five can change the world."

CRIME

Along with worries over public schools, fear of crime probably keeps more people out of cities like Flint and Detroit than anything else. And like education, crime elicits a vast array of suggestions for curing this ill, from technological fixes (like putting sound-monitoring devices in crime-ridden neighborhoods to detect and pinpoint the location of gunshots so police can respond more quickly) to organizational or administrative reforms—more community policing, more federal money for cops on the street, decriminalization of marijuana, and much more.

One of my personal experiences with crime hints at a solution. One Sunday afternoon a few years ago, my wife and I attended an Urban Land Institute conference at Detroit's Cobo Center convention facility. We parked our minivan on a downtown street adjacent to Cobo, and we came out a couple of hours later to find a side window smashed and one of our bicycles stolen out of the back. It was an unpleasant experience, and seemed doubly unfair (I know this is somewhat irrational) considering that we weren't some naïve out-of-towners but city residents committed to bettering our urban space. I don't think more police would have prevented that crime; there are only so many places the cops can be at any one moment. Nor would technology necessarily have prevented the break-in, although more surveillance cameras might have helped catch the thief. What might have helped, and what may yet help cities everywhere, is the sum total of the policies and tactics explored in this book, which might be summed up by the simple phrase "lively streets."

The great urban writer Jane Jacobs knew this a half-century ago. She told us in the 1960s in her *Death and Life of Great American Cities* that the more people on our sidewalks, the more eyes watching the pavement, the safer our streets will be. Jacobs drew her lessons from her neighborhood in lower Manhattan, but as we'll see later in more detail, that same idea is in operation in places like the Brightmoor neighborhood in Detroit, where a woman named Riet Schumack and her neighbors have used community gardens to discourage drug houses and prostitution, and in the work of a Detroit artist named Mitch Cope, whose efforts to nurture a burgeoning artists' enclave helps to drive out the bad guys. Streets that are empty are more likely to have criminals roaming them than streets filled with pedestrians and shoppers and bicyclists. The day the thief broke into our minivan there was nobody in sight walking around that part of downtown Detroit, either when we parked or when we returned to our vehicle.

Now, I am the first to admit the problem of urban crime goes far beyond some yuppies getting their bicycles ripped off. The scourge of homicide, rape, and other violent felonies is a bottomless tragedy scarring millions of lives. These violent crimes plague the citizens least able to defend themselves—the very young, the very old, the ones so poor they lack the money and skills to find a better place to live.

But iron bars on our windows cannot stop this plague. We need to change society itself, and we do that by creating better cities. The commitment may require what William James called "the moral equivalent of war." Perhaps first we must understand that by throwing away our legacy cities we create implacable problems for ourselves.

So, at the risk of simplification, the key to a healthier city is, well, a healthier city. The more we make the sort of improvements we've been exploring in this book—more efficient governance structures, better schools, and the more entrepreneurial business models and new land uses that we'll turn to next— the more we do all these things, the more people will find our cities safe and attractive places to live and work and play. It takes awhile to get there. But eventually the sum total of the changes will begin to help. And we may then experience a virtuous cycle as opposed to a vicious one, with each new benefit leading to more and more of the same.

ECONOMICS

GROWING NEW ECONOMIC MODELS

In 2009, a twenty-six-year-old photography buff named Rick DeVos came up with an intriguing way to spend some of his family's fortune (an Amway inheritance from the company co-founded by his grandfather). Young DeVos believed that art of all kinds—painting, photography, drama, film, music—generates a unique chemistry between creators and consumers within the public realm; and with that in mind, he hoped to create some sort of art event that would enliven the downtown of his native Grand Rapids, Michigan. He thought first of sponsoring a film festival, but decided *his* festival might get lost amid all the others out there; besides, he wanted something more yeasty than having people sit in the dark for a couple of hours and discuss the films later. He was searching for "something that we could do that's completely different and that still has this conversational quality and this buzz." DeVos had been interested in the notion of art prizes, and in talking with others he came up with the idea of holding the world's biggest open art competition, with the public at large voting for the winner instead of a select jury making the awards. And so ArtPrize was born.

What seized the media's attention was the size of the top prize—$250,000 for the winner selected by the general public. (DeVos family money backstopped the event, but it also drew wide support from foundations and other donors.) But the rules, too, were fresh and different. Any artist in the world could enter, and anyone with property in downtown Grand Rapids could host a work of art. Any and all visitors could vote on their favorite artwork. That first year, ArtPrize ran for eighteen days, featuring more than twelve hundred artists and 159 venues through the city, including parking garages and the empty floors of downtown office buildings. Artists from forty-one states and fourteen countries were

Rick DeVos. (Photo courtesy of ArtPrize)

represented. More than three hundred thousand votes were tallied. The winner, a Brooklyn artist named Ran Ortner, won for his large-scale painting of oceanic waves called *Open Water No. 24*. ArtPrize grew even bigger in the following years.

Okay, so why begin a chapter on economics by talking about art? Because the dollars-and-cents impact on downtown Grand Rapids was huge. There were so many visitors that restaurants ran out of food, and hotels turned away visitors for lack of rooms. On the final day of the event, the line to see Ortner's winning work stretched down two city blocks. In its third year, the 2011 ArtPrize pumped $15.4 million into the Grand Rapids economy, according to an impact study done by the Anderson Economic Group, a consulting firm from East Lansing, Michigan; that year, the event drew more than 320,000 visitors and

Thousands throng the streets of Grand Rapids for the 2009 ArtPrize. (Courtesy of Art-Prize)

created an estimated two hundred new jobs during its nineteen-day run. "The economic impact of ArtPrize is considerable, especially for an event that is still in its infancy," said Scott Watkins, a senior consultant with AEG. "Our study shows locals and visitors alike spend money at area businesses that might not otherwise attract them as customers."

If art can produce jobs and revenue, cities like Grand Rapids will take it. All our older industrial cities will do the same. As a young reporter back in the late '70s, I worked for a few years in Rochester, New York, at a time when Eastman Kodak, the "Great Yellow Father" (so called for its yellow film boxes) employed some sixty thousand workers there; as I write this in early 2012, Kodak employs fewer than seven thousand workers in Rochester, and having just filed for bankruptcy, no doubt will employ fewer still. When Youngstown, Ohio, was a capital of world steel production in the 1970s, some 180,000 people called Youngstown home; then the mills closed, and today fewer than seventy thousand people live there. General Motors once employed eighty thousand workers in Flint, Michigan; today it employs perhaps a tenth that number. Leipzig, Germany, as we'll see later, lost ninety percent of its industrial jobs almost overnight after German reunification. Detroit in 1972, as we saw earlier,

Artist Ortner's winning entry for the 2009 ArtPrize. (Courtesy of ArtPrize)

was home to 2,398 manufacturing facilities employing 180,000 workers, or about twelve percent of the city's population. By 2007, the Census Bureau found just 472 facilities employing 22,962 workers, or only about three percent of the city's residents. This vaporization of America's manufacturing base has devastated hundreds of towns and cities.

Nobody asserts that a few art events would ever make up for those losses. But as communities try to reimagine their economies, they are looking to art along with much else. Just as we accept that the model of municipal government is broken and needs replacing, so, too, must our economic models in these communities be replaced. Anything that offers hope gets a serious hearing, including things previously overlooked in economic development like art and cultural events.

In a few cases, art has transformed communities. We'll briefly look at two: Stratford, Ontario, and Lancaster, Pennsylvania.

In the early 1950s, Stratford was a sleepy town in southwest Ontario, abandoned by the railroads that had underpinned its economy for eighty years. A journalist named Tom Patterson, trying to find a new basis for that economy, campaigned to create a Shakespeare theater festival on the banks of the town's Avon River. A giant tent was imported from Chicago to house the first productions. British actor and director Tyrone Guthrie agreed to serve as the festival's first artistic director. The festival's inaugural presentation, a production of *Richard III*, opened on July 13, 1953, with Alec Guinness in the title role. Success built on success; over the years, actors including Julie Harris, Christopher Plummer, Brian Dennehy, Maggie Smith, Jason Robards, and Peter Ustinov performed at Stratford. Today the Stratford Festival enjoys an annual operating budget of just under sixty million dollars and employs more than a thousand people. With a season running from April to November and plays presented at five distinct stages, the festival also offers tours, concerts, lectures, discussions, and author appearances. Thousands of students attend educational enrichment programs. The Birmingham Conservatory for Classical Theatre offers training for aspiring theater professionals. And all because the town of Stratford needed to reimagine its economy after industry pulled out.

More briefly, Lancaster, nestled in the heart of Amish country in south-central Pennsylvania, understood in recent years that the many tourists who passed through to see Amish sites weren't stopping in Lancaster itself. So the city deliberately set out to promote its downtown as a shopping hub, with dozens of art galleries and boutiques opening in recent years. Perhaps not by coincidence, Lancaster's population, which peaked in the 1950s at about sixty-four thousand but dipped to fifty-four thousand by 1980, grew about five percent percent in the first decade of the 2000s.

Art concerns itself primarily with matters of the soul and spirit, not jobs and tax bases. But when communities are desperate, art seems like a pretty good way to go. A 2012 report called Creative State Michigan, released by ArtServe Michigan, the state's leading cultural advocacy organization, found that 211 arts and cultural organizations had contributed nearly five hundred million dollars to the Michigan economy in 2009—in the same year that General Motors and Chrysler were filing for bankruptcy. Art and culture revenue included $152 million paid out in salaries for 15,560 jobs. From 2006 to 2010, the number of arts-related jobs increased by four percent in Michigan, and arts-related businesses increased by forty-three percent—again while overall job numbers in the state were in free fall. "As Michigan has sought methods to overcome its economic challenges, the creative industries largely have been overlooked, despite the significant value they bring to the state's economy," said Jennifer Goulet, president and CEO of ArtServe. Among the culture world's contributions, she added, was its ability to attract and retain well-educated professionals and business investment.

Rick DeVos wasn't thinking of remaking the state's economy when he created ArtPrize in Grand Rapids. He mostly just wanted to have some fun and shake things up. But the results point to just one way in which new and inventive approaches can replace a piece of our lost industrial base—a tiny piece, perhaps, but still worthwhile.

"I consider myself an entrepreneur," DeVos told me in early 2012. "It really comes down to trying to provoke folks to try stuff and do things."

In city after city—certainly in Youngstown and Detroit and Rochester and more—it took a long time for people to admit that the old economy had vanished, and that it wasn't coming back. In places like Flint, Michigan, birthplace of General Motors, where the sit-down strikers of the 1930s gave rise to the modern union movement, the automotive culture was everything. Dan Kildee, the innovative former treasurer of the county and proponent of the modern land bank, recalls growing up in that culture. "I'm from Flint," he said in a 2011 discussion. "There was a time when we knew with absolute certainty that we would continue to have high employment, really good paying jobs, because we were exporting cars across the globe and importing cash. And we knew with the kind of certainty that ought to frighten anybody who feels this way, we knew that it would never end."

End it did, in hundreds of places large and small, from the coalfields of eastern Pennsylvania to the Soviet-supported industrial cities of the old European Eastern Bloc to the steel and rubber and chemical and automotive cities of America's Rust Belt. By now, just about everyone accepts that there is no magic formula, no innovative tax credit, no glitzy marketing campaign that will fill up all the factories and the empty houses and take us back to those magic years of the 1950s. Everyone, for better or worse, accepts we must try something new.

That "new" thing in many cases is entrepreneurship—a homegrown approach to business growth that promotes small start-up ventures as the eventual replacement for the lost auto and steel and other industrial jobs.

The effort goes by various names, including "economic gardening," as in nurturing your homegrown efforts rather than prospecting elsewhere. Not every community will produce the next Bill Gates or Steve Jobs, but of course successful entrepreneurial start-ups number in the many thousands across the nation, and produce great numbers of new jobs. To help that process along, many communities have launched "business incubators," also known as "business accelerators." These incubators vary from place to place, but as a general rule they provide cheap office or laboratory space, shared clerical and other business services, mentoring by business coaches, perhaps a line on investment capital, and—most importantly—an encouraging atmosphere where entrepreneurs can find networking and advice from others like themselves occupying the next cubicle.

The growth of the incubator concept has been phenomenal. The primary trade group for the field, the US–based National Business Incubation Association, estimates that there are about seven thousand incubators worldwide, including more than fourteen hundred in North America, up from only twelve in 1980. Many of these are in places you might think wouldn't need them—Northern California, say, where they've become part of the rich ecosystem of the tech world—part of that network of talent spotters and investors so important in the digital community. Today many Old Economy communities see incubators operating within their borders. Detroit's TechTown, the business accelerator based at Wayne State University, opened in 2004. Ann Arbor SPARK, a multipart economic development agency that includes a business accelerator, started shortly afterward. The Macomb Oakland University Incubator in suburban Detroit opened its doors in late 2011. And there are incubators in Kalamazoo and Lansing and many other communities in Michigan as well as throughout the American heartland. The NBIA estimates that business accelerators in North America nurtured over 35,000 start-ups, and have launched roughly 19,500 graduate companies.

Some companies that emerge from incubators fit the image of high-tech start-ups on the way to something big. Many others are much smaller firms in a variety of fields, including food service, educational counseling, energy auditing, and much more. At TechTown, among the more promising firms as of early 2012 were companies that were developing a low-cost, radiation-free screen for breast cancer (Angott Medical Products); creating biofueling stations for alternative fuels at truck stops and fleet centers (Clean Emission Fluids); and working on an ignition system that promises to increase fuel efficiency for fleet vehicles (ENRG Power Systems). Almost any accelerator in the nation would offer as much variety.

Randal Charlton, a British-born entrepreneur whose biotechnology company Asterand became TechTown's first tenant firm and who later became president of the incubator, likes to preach the importance of the collegial ambience at a good accelerator. "You've got to have a culture of entrepreneurship," Charlton told me in one of our many conversations. "Our challenge is not to disperse people with great entrepreneurial skills. It's to keep them close together because we've got to build this culture and knowledge of managed risk-taking. And that's key to it. I can't emphasize that enough."

We should not, of course, too quickly write off the Old Economy as we celebrate the New. Manufacturing remains of huge importance in places like Detroit; indeed, the Brookings Institution estimates that metro Detroit leads the nation's 20 largest cities in terms of the percentage of its total economic output that it exports beyond the borders of the US (largely auto parts). Manufacturing no longer resembles its "smokestack" image; today the most rudimentary jobs in auto plants require at least an associate's degree, and the factories themselves (and the cars coming out of them) are cleaner and more high-tech than ever. Innovative manufacturing creates well-paying jobs, spurs research and development, nurtures entrepreneurial spin-offs, and helps give the US the technological edge that it holds to this day. Bruce Katz, a Brookings vice president and director of its Metropolitan Policy Program, suggests that the US wasted a generation chasing the mirage of a post-manufacturing economy, one based solely on debt-fueled real-estate expansion and financial speculation. A chastened nation may now be returning to a saner, safer economy based on production, innovation, and exports. "That's a pretty good platform to build off of," he told me in early 2012. "The pre-recession economy literally was an Arizona economy—build a lot of homes, build a lot of big-box retail, maybe generate a lot of ideas, but the production would happen abroad. The post-recession economy could be a Michigan economy."

That's sound advice, although it sometimes leads to a simplistic variation that holds that cities like Detroit simply need a CEO-led strategy, a view that holds that cities will revive only when leaders of the largest corporations adopt a town, create jobs, and underwrite major showcase projects. A wealth of evidence contradicts that notion. CEOs play their part, but so do entrepreneurs, university researchers, nonprofit activists, civic leaders—really everyone who pitches in to help cities. To rely solely on CEOs for a city's revival is to miss the rich broth of economic alternatives bubbling up from below.

If cities like Youngstown and Flint and Detroit haven't yet reaped as many benefits as they might from their entrepreneurial start-ups, we might trace that to the lack of a true entrepreneurial culture in these cities. Cities in Pennsylvania and Ohio and Wisconsin and other industrial belt states have relied so heavily for so long on the giant-corporation model that's it has taken civic and business leaders, not to mention ordinary folks, a long time to learn new habits. I cherish the story of the long-established corporate chieftains in Pittsburgh who finally decided in the 1980s to make peace with some of the more entrepreneurial upstarts in town, inviting them to the fabled Duquesne Club for a get-acquainted dinner. But when the evening came, none of the new "tech guys" could get in, for they weren't wearing ties, as club rules demanded.

So what does an entrepreneurial culture look and feel like? Skip Simms, senior vice president at Ann Arbor SPARK, told me in 2011 that creative young people flock to a place like Silicon Valley expecting serial careers; they're not only *willing* to work for a succession of high-tech companies, they're *looking* for that type of career in a spirit of risk-taking and reinvention. By contrast, the model in Rust Belt cities for so long was to join GM/Kodak/Dow/US Steel early and hang on like grim death until retirement. Another reason why Chicago or San Francisco continues to attract so many young people is that those cities offer the safety net of many employers in many fields, all of which need talent. In a place like Detroit or Flint, the choices more often seem much narrower, and thus the desire to land sometime secure for the long term.

How people treat success in an entrepreneurial hotbed proves equally instructive. In a true entrepreneurial culture, Simms told me at SPARK during my visit, if someone makes a fortune in one venture, he or she plows the money back into the next, and not as a passive investor, either, but as someone who wants to be deeply involved. "Whereas here," Simms said, "I make a couple million bucks, what am I doing with it? I'm giving it to Goldman Sachs or somebody else to manage for me, or I buy the Fortune 500 stock. The idea of taking that money and putting it at high risk with an unknown quantity known as a start-up is foreign here."

One way to measure the entrepreneurial culture is to look to data provided by the Kauffman Foundation, a Kansas City nonprofit that studies entrepreneurship. That data are less than encouraging at this point for Rust Belt economies. Kauffman estimated that Michigan had about 250 entrepreneurs per hundred thousand residents in 2010, a level that ranked Michigan thirty-third out of the fifty states. Ohio did a little better; there were three hundred entrepreneurs per hundred thousand people in the state. But the Rust Belt lags behind Sunbelt states Georgia and Nevada, each of which had 510 entrepreneurs per hundred thousand residents, making them the nation's leading states for entrepreneurial activity. Kauffman also ranks metro areas; metro Detroit ranked twelfth out of the fifteen largest metropolitan areas for entrepreneurial activity, lagging behind such metro areas as Los Angeles, Houston, Miami, and Atlanta.

Another indicator is the number of venture capital deals done in various parts of the nation, reported by the National Venture Capital Association. The group reported that venture capital deals in the Midwest in 2011 totaled $1.4 billion. Venture deals in Silicon Valley that same year totaled more than eight times as much. For Michigan by itself, the numbers seem paltry. Venture deals in the state peaked in 2000 with fifty-five deals totaling $286 million in equity investments. But that number dwindled during the recent recession and its aftermath. During 2010, Michigan saw thirty-three deals worth $152 million.

I point out these data not to discourage Rust Belt entrepreneurs, but merely to say that cities like Detroit and Flint and Youngstown and Rochester have just begun their transitions from an economy based on one huge industry and giant corporations to an economy based on individual entrepreneurship. The employment gains so far remain modest, even hard to measure in the government's monthly employment reports. Surveys of the labor market "often miss these little guys," says Charles Ballard, a professor of economics at Michigan State University. "The little guy who has a good idea and makes something in his garage and has one employee, that person is often under the radar screen."

But if the shoots of this entrepreneurial flowering remain fragile, they grow stronger by the year. And the promise is huge.

In downtown Detroit, businessman Dan Gilbert, the founder and chairman of the Quicken Loans online mortgage company, has been buying historic office buildings since he moved his own company downtown in 2010; most of his buildings were either empty or only partially occupied when he bought them. He gave them a high-energy makeover, with a stated goal of nurturing a more entrepreneurial economy based on digital technology in downtown Detroit. He called his concept Detroit 2.0, and he dubbed the city's Woodward Avenue "Webward Avenue" to make his point. Nowhere was that effort more visible or more promising than in a modest fifty-thousand-square-foot building on the edge of downtown that Gilbert rechristened the M@dison.

Built in 1917 as the Madison Theatre Building, the structure stood empty for many years before Gilbert and his partners bought it. He gave it a top-to-bottom remake in a style best described as industrial chic—leaving the original concrete floors, steel beams, and industrial ceiling tiles exposed, and filling the wide-open spaces with edgy furniture and graphics. He rented one floor to a graphic design company called Skidmore Studio, another to his own investment firm, Detroit Venture Partners (DVP), and other space to entrepreneurial start-ups funded by DVP. The workers who fill up the M@dison have tended to be youthful, casually dressed, versed in the latest digital creative design technology, and committed to the downtown lifestyle.

Skidmore Studio moved from its suburban location downtown to the M@dison to be part of the emerging culture. Tim Smith, president and CEO of Skidmore, told me in early 2012 that the work product his team produced got better once they made the move in fall 2011. "I have twenty-five creative folks who work here," he said. "Their creative energy is really built on the emotion that goes with it. And once we were down here, the work elevated itself because of the emotion of being here. . . . To have a client say, 'You guys were always good, but now I'm seeing a whole different level of work,' that's a very rewarding thing."

Josh Linkner, Gilbert's friend and the managing partner of Detroit Venture

Here at the M@dison in downtown Detroit, a new incubator for digital start-ups caters to young creatives. (Author photo)

Partners, said the firm had looked at hundreds of potential start-ups and funded about a dozen by early 2012. All were in digital technology, and virtually none of them had anything to do with the city's twentieth-century signature industry—the automotive field. A typical venture was a small Web-based entrant called Are You a Human? The firm took a simple idea—that consumers hate filling out those squiggly letters as a security check during online shopping—and created a game-based human authentication platform. The games can be customized for a variety of brand messages. Linkner said that Gilbert and his partners (who include basketball legend Magic Johnson) hope, naturally enough, for some big winners to emerge from their pool of start-ups. He pointed to the success of the online discount shopping aide Groupon as a role model. "Groupon in three years created over ten thousand jobs," Linkner said. "If we have a couple hits, not even of that magnitude but reasonable hits, that's going to start to say something pretty big about this region."

With Gilbert plunging so much money into his portfolio of historic office buildings—over one hundred million dollars by most estimates—he has been

The Green Garage in Detroit's Midtown district began life as a Model T showroom and assembly space. Today the building is a showcase of environmental sustainability, from the salvaged wood used for desks and tables to the many energy-saving practices and technologies. (Author photo)

banking on values in the historically depressed downtown Detroit market taking a healthy turn upward. But as Linkner said, an investment in the M@dison—twelve million dollars to buy and renovate the building—was not a real-estate play in the usual sense. "This building doesn't make economic sense yet," Linkner told me. "This is not a high-profit real-estate deal here. This is a commitment to entrepreneurship in Detroit."

When I visit places like the M@dison and TechTown and Ann Arbor SPARK—or similar entrepreneurial hubs that I've seen in Manchester, England, and Leipzig, Germany (more on that later)—it's hard not to believe that something new and profoundly important is happening in our older industrial cities. The energy arising from all these hundreds of start-up firms, the enthusiasm of their young workers, the sense of being almost totally unconcerned with the past and its problems—all these aspects speak of an entrepreneurial movement that has leaped a generation ahead.

Of course, even true believers in this movement have to admit that the number of new jobs created by all these incubators and start-up firms remains modest, at least in most of the older industrial cities. As Professor Ballard of MSU says, most of these firms don't show up in the macroeconomic surveys of the labor market, so it's hard to judge their impact. And it will take an awful lot of these efforts to dent the huge losses a state like Michigan has suffered in recent years—losing about eight hundred thousand jobs in all during the 2000s and half of its manufacturing jobs in a ten-year span ending in 2011. In our enthusiasm, we should not expect miracles.

But a visit to a place like the M@dison or TechTown provides a bracing antidote to the despair one may feel visiting some of Detroit's abandoned places. Whatever else is happening in Detroit and other industrial cities, a great many very smart young people are creating something new. That something new may be the economy of the future.

"It's early on, but we're super optimistic," Linkner said. "We're talking about adding thousands of high-tech workers here in the city over the next ten years, about filling over a million square feet of office space and creating over a billion dollars of economic impact here in Detroit. So to us the game has just begun, but we're sprinting toward success."

The art economy and business incubators are just two of the new-economy initiatives our legacy cities are exploring. Among the others:

IMMIGRATION

If there's any city whose success testifies to the economic benefits of immigration, that city was the Detroit of the twentieth century.

From German-born architect Albert Kahn, who helped create the modern industrial age with his innovative factory designs for Henry Ford, to the tidal influx of workers from many lands who toiled in the auto plants for successive generations, immigrants powered Detroit's rise to prominence. One might even make a circumstantial case that Detroit's fall from grace was due in part to—or at least accompanied—a period of reduced immigration. A 2008 report from the Brookings Institution noted that in 1900, on the eve of the city's explosive growth, thirty-four percent of Detroit's population was foreign-born. By 1970, as the city's decline accelerated, immigrants' share of the city's population had fallen to 7.1 percent.

Today, promoting Detroit and other cities as immigrant-friendly environments represents for many advocates one way out of a city's deep economic hole. Fans of immigration point to success stories like Vinay Gupta, who grew up in New Delhi, India, and came to the US to get his MBA from the University of Michigan. He and a partner formed BlueGill Technologies, a highly successful start-up firm in Ann Arbor, and later Gupta went on to run a succession of other entrepreneurial ventures, including a software firm called Janeeva. Gupta's advice to cities like Detroit: Transform yourselves into more livable places. Immigrants, especially foreign students, "are used to living in big cities. They don't want to move to suburbia."

Among those listening is Michigan Governor Rick Snyder, who has urged his fellow state residents to help retain foreign students who come to Michigan to earn advanced degrees and then go home. Michigan should do more to keep them, Snyder has said publicly many times. "Immigration made us a great state and country," Snyder told interviewers in early 2012. "It is time we embrace this concept as a way to speed our reinvention."

A nonprofit effort called Global Detroit, led by a former state representative named Steve Tobocman, who served three terms in Lansing from the Latino district in Southwest Detroit, released a study in 2011 that promoted eleven steps to attract entrepreneurial immigrants. The recommendations are aimed at Michigan and particularly at Detroit, but they make sense for any distressed post-industrial city. Among the ideas:

Create and support an EB-5 investor visa regional center. The EB-5 investor visa program allows foreign investors who invest one million dollars in an American business that creates ten jobs to receive permanent legal residency for themselves and their immediate family. Global Detroit recommends ramping up efforts to attract those investors.

Do more to attract and retain foreign students at local universities. With over twenty-three thousand foreign students injecting nearly six hundred million dollars annually into the state, Michigan's foreign student population ranks as the eighth largest in the country. Linking those students to prospective employers and otherwise working to keep these talented newcomers in the state could mean a big economic payoff down the line.

Strive to be an attractive "second landing" spot for immigrants. Global Detroit estimates that one-third of Michigan's foreign-born residents came to the state from somewhere else in the US. As an example, large numbers of Bangladeshi immigrants have relocated to the Detroit area from Queens, New York. Global Detroit recommends reaching out to existing ethnic groups to help them see the city as a welcoming environment.

Create a Mayor's Office of Global Affairs. This office would serve as liaison and ambassador to ethnic and foreign-born communities. The "welcome mat" services could include job training and placement, immigration law services, and English-language classes.

"Immigrants have been huge job creators," Tobocman said. "We ought to be looking at everything we can to create the kind of Michigan we had in the twentieth century."

Other cities have equally caught on to the benefits of immigration. In Manchester, England, economic development officials welcome immigrants with the slogan: "It's not where you're from, it's where you're at."

THE BLUE ECONOMY

In recent years, a simple fact has set people thinking in Great Lakes cities like Milwaukee and Detroit. The five Great Lakes contain twenty percent of the world's fresh water. Michigan's portion of the Great Lakes alone holds more water by volume than Saudi Arabia has oil. In an ever-thirstier world, could that resource be turned to our economic advantage?

"The Great Lakes are our economic ace in the hole," Tim Eder, executive director of the nonprofit Great Lakes Commission, a coalition of US and Canadian interests, told me in 2011. "The water is going to provide the lubricant to make our economy hum."

In recent years, entrepreneurs and civic leaders have been trying in many ways to encourage the creation of a blue economy—developing technology to purify water, recycle it, measure how clean or dirty it is, and to provide water-based expertise to the world. The market for water technology is estimated at five hundred billion dollars a year and growing.

"We're sitting on liquid gold," Dave Egner, director of the New Economy Initiative, a coalition of nonprofit foundations hoping to steer Michigan toward a new economic future, said in a 2011 interview.

Developing water-related technologies tends to be expensive. Funding for pilot programs is scarce, and big water users, such as public water departments, tend to be conservative and reluctant to try something new. As a result, many economists and entrepreneurs say the state is not nearly as aggressive as it could be about leveraging its water for growth.

"This isn't a tree-hugger argument," said John Austin, a fellow of the Brookings Institution who has written extensively on water. "This is about creating more jobs and economic development in Detroit and Milwaukee and Cleveland, where we need it."

"Our interest is in creating jobs," Egner agreed. "We've got to draw attention to this resource, and we haven't done it."

University researchers across Michigan are working on many aspects of the problem, dealing with everything from protecting water resources from invasive species, such as Asian carp, to studying the amount of sediment building up behind local dams.

Meanwhile, the private sector is finding an international market for smart water-related products. Cascade Engineering, a longtime supplier of plastic parts to the automotive and furniture industries, has developed a simple plastic water purification product for use by individual households in developing nations. Based in Grand Rapids, Cascade said its HydrAidBioSand filter weighs only eight pounds empty, is easily installed, and can provide safe water for eight to ten people a day. The company plans to manufacture and distribute three hundred thousand filters, along with initiating education efforts on the health benefits of clean water.

"There are eight hundred million people who do not have regular access to a safe water supply," said Christina Keller, business unit leader for Cascade. Meeting such an essential need is good for the people it helps and good for the company's bottom line, too.

UNIVERSITIES

An invention a day.

That's how the University of Michigan's Tech Transfer office—the folks responsible for commercializing the incredible research done across so many fields at UM—characterizes the wealth of innovation at the school. More concretely, the Tech Transfer office can point to eleven start-up firms born of university research in 2011. The number appears to be picking up—eleven start-ups in 2010–11, compared to ten in 2009–10 and eight in 2008–09. Among the recent winners: a firm called Csquared Innovations, which developed a plasma deposition process used to apply coatings on everything from jet turbines and nonstick frying pans to batteries and solar panels. Another winner: Compendia Bioscience Inc., which developed a DNA database that allows pharmaceutical companies to screen potential drug compounds against 240 cell lines in targeted, cost-effective clinical trials, shortening the time to market. These firms may or may not score big in the wider world of technology and the stock market, but their initial success promises good things.

This sort of work has not gone unnoticed among the broader business and economic development world. As the economy crumbled in recent years, in Detroit and in so many other places, more and more people began to try to link university research—valued at more than one billion dollars a year at UM in Ann Arbor alone—to regional efforts at economic revival. It's part of a broader networking of universities, foundations, industry, and government to get the most out of any and all assets.

In early 2012, UM led the creation of the Tech Transfer Talent Network, an effort by seven state universities to increase the supply of entrepreneurs and mentors who can lend their expertise to university tech transfer offices. Among other things, it includes a database of people willing to serve as mentors, consultants, and even owners and partners in the commercialization of university research. UM also offers a Mentors-in-Residence program, in which experienced entrepreneurs serve twelve-to-eighteen-month rotations in the Tech Transfer office to assess new possibilities and offer advice to start-up ventures.

"Most people agree that the core problem holding back economic vitality is having available talent, especially in the Midwest. We aim to change that," said Ken Nisbet, executive director of UM Tech Transfer.

These tech transfer offices at universities serve another important purpose beyond spawning start-up firms. Often, Nisbet told me during an interview, the job is to feed innovations into existing companies, strengthening the state's economy in that way. Often this role assumes greater importance than spinning off new companies. During 2011, UM signed 101 licensing agreements for its technology while also spinning off the eleven start-up firms that year. For city and state economies looking for a revival, it's all good.

Now, with cities trying to reinvent themselves, many universities are working out ways to get promising research out of the lab and into the marketplace more quickly. Schools on the West Coast and in the Northeast have done this better than others; but recently universities in distressed areas of the nation, including the industrial heartland, are more actively promoting business growth by tapping into their own research. UM now has thirty people working in its Tech Transfer office, and Wayne State University not long ago linked its own technology transfer office more directly to its TechTown business incubator.

Many of the university researchers pronounced themselves happy to help. UM engineering professor Pravansu Mohanty, founder of the Csquared plasma-coating firm, believes in what he calls the concept-to-component approach to research: "My Edisonian belief is that innovation should ideally lead to a product, which will in turn generate revenue, which can then be used to fund more innovative research."

And Perry Samson, a professor of atmospheric, oceanic, and space sciences in UM's College of Engineering, has his LectureTools Web-based study program registered at more than one hundred colleges around the world. The program allows students to take quizzes, synchronize their notes with lecture slides, submit questions, and otherwise interact with their professors. UM's Tech Transfer office helped him get the program into the marketplace. "This kind of entrepreneurship is good for the economy, good for the city, and good for the students," Samson says.

And Hankan Oral, a professor of internal medicine at UM's Medical School, started a company called Ablation Frontiers, later acquired by Medtronic, that is commercializing a process that makes treatment of blood clots easier.

"The environment has never been better for faculty who want to pursue their entrepreneurial dreams," Oral said.

WHAT ROLE FOR GOVERNMENT?

As an alternative or supplement to entrepreneurial efforts, some voices advocate government playing more of a role in the economy. Ironically, these voices can be either progressives (who favor a government industrial policy backing favored industries, such as green energy) or conservatives (who want government to weaken unions and subsidize their own favored industries, such as oil and mineral extraction). Certainly a government with its thumb on the scale can help or hurt; the federal rescue of bankrupt General Motors and Chrysler in 2009 saved an entire industrial sector. But government policy runs to the fickle, and cities have learned the hard way not to rely on either state or federal largesse.

A case study: In 2008, the State of Michigan approved the nation's most generous incentives for moviemakers. Filmmakers could get back up to forty-two percent of their expenses for shooting in Michigan—a bonus so lucrative that it guaranteed two things: that moviemakers would flock to the state in numbers never seen there before, and, second, that the state would lose money on the deal. Certainly it worked, in the most basic sense of attracting film productions. For a heady eighteen months or so, we got used to seeing film crews and their sets all around the city of Detroit. The media recorded sightings of Clint Eastwood (filming *Gran Torino*), Al Pacino (*You Don't Know Jack*), George Clooney (*The Ides of March*), Hilary Swank (*Conviction*), and many others. A handful of permanent movie production houses appeared ready to open, although most were underfunded and some got no further than a hopeful press release. I even heard of film crews buying expensive camera equipment in metro Detroit to qualify for the state's forty-two percent credit and selling it for a big profit back in L.A. Soon, conservative lawmakers in Lansing were battling to strip away the windfall to producers; and when Governor Rick Snyder took office in early 2011, he and the legislature did just that, reducing the pool of money available to just a fraction of what it had been. Detroit's and the state's brief moment as Hollywood Midwest ended, and the moviemakers moved on to other states willing to pony up more money. Draw what conclusion you will, but to offer such a generous benefit, get everyone's hopes up, get people to commit real money to the state, and then yank it all away two years later—that did nobody any good.

As for some of the other prescriptions that politicians present, such as right-to-work legislation as a cure-all for a weak business climate, those are better left on the cutting-room floor. In the 1950s and '60s, when Michigan enjoyed personal income levels well above the national average, it ranked among the most unionized states in the nation. Its unions have shrunk a good deal since then, but Michigan still leads many other states in the percentage of residents carrying union cards, even as its income levels have sunk well below the national average. The only thing that matters is how innovative your economic actors are in the face of continuous change and challenge.

THE WAY AHEAD

Skip Simms of Ann Arbor SPARK likes to say that Henry Ford failed twice before he succeeded. "That means he had three rounds of investors before he finally hit on the one that worked," he told me. As a pithy anecdote, that captures much that our cities are trying to capture today—remembering their great legacy of past invention, even as they nurture those energetic innovators who take failure as part of success and who expect their journey to be anything but boringly smooth. Places like Rochester and Flint and Youngstown and Detroit may have a long, long way to go yet. But the journey is underway.

"I have no illusions that we'll ever be like Silicon Valley," Simms told me, "but at least if we can get a significant portion of those people thinking that way that didn't think that way five years ago, let alone ten years ago, that's going to move the needle quickly for our entrepreneurs."

5

NEW USES FOR URBAN LAND

TURNING VACANCY TO GOOD USE

Detroiters have engaged in a lively debate in recent years over "ruin porn," the depiction by photographers of the city's empty factories, burned-out houses, crumbing commercial buildings, and other sad reminders of a lost urban era. Many photographers offer their painful images with high-sounding rhetoric; they compare Detroit to ancient Rome, or issue warnings on the failures of capitalism, or celebrate the robust ability of nature to retake its domain the moment Man steps out of the picture. I acknowledge the technical skill of many of these photographers, even as I dislike much of their output. To cite just one, the photographs in Andrew Moore's *Detroit Disassembled* strike me as too voyeuristic, the photos themselves so hyper-detailed and color saturated as to seem artificial—Photoshopped to perfection, perhaps. Mostly I dislike ruin porn because the genre misses the two most important aspects of Detroit today. First, it misses the vitality still found in many parts of Detroit. Midtown with its creative young people, Southwest Detroit with its Latino immigrants, the Gold Coast with its elegant architecture—ruin porn misses all these. Ruin porn gives the impression that no one lives in Detroit anymore, but I personally have joined thousands of bicyclists for the annual *Tour de Troit* ride through city streets; waited on long lines to see the latest blockbuster show at the Detroit Institute of Arts; strolled along the riverfront on a busy Sunday afternoon with thousands of others. Ruin porn misses all this, just as it misses the other most striking feature of Detroit today (an unpardonable lapse given its importance to the city's future)—the city's vast amount of vacant land.

By vacant land I mean just that—empty fields, land going back to nature, overgrown with the tall grasses of a neglected urban space. Counting all the vacant lots in the city along with parks that the city government can no longer or only rarely maintain and the untraveled streets filled with trash in abandoned neighborhoods, almost forty square miles of Detroit's 139-square-mile geographic footprint now stands vacant. How much is forty square miles? We could drop the city of Paris, France, into a space that big. If we resettled that much land using the population density of Chicago today, we'd add another half-million residents to Detroit. Forty square miles is a lot of vacancy. And while some experts prefer a more conservative estimate closer to twenty square miles (counting only those parcels from which buildings have been removed and leaving out even the trash-strewn streets and unkempt parks), there is no disagreement that the vacancy in Detroit is huge—and growing.

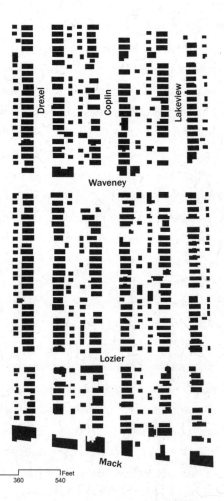

A figure-ground image depicts the footprints of all the buildings in a dense Detroit neighborhood in 1949. (Courtesy of Eric Dueweke, University of Michigan)

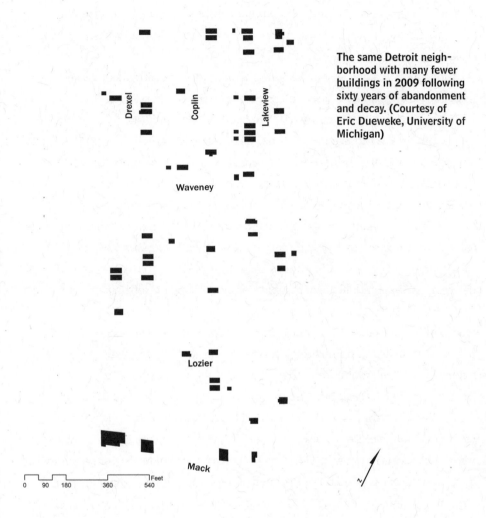

The same Detroit neighborhood with many fewer buildings in 2009 following sixty years of abandonment and decay. (Courtesy of Eric Dueweke, University of Michigan)

Now, to put that in perspective, consider: We often think of suburbia as bustling and Detroit as empty, but in fact the suburbs today feature *more* vacant land than Detroit—more land, that is, upon which no structures stand. Suburban vacancy, though, is purposely vacant—generous setbacks in residential subdivisions, very wide medians on main suburban thoroughfares, buffer zones around malls and office parks. Even today, Detroit's population density is roughly twice that of its suburbs, just as it is twice the density of spread-out Sunbelt cities like Phoenix and Houston, which sprawl over so many hundreds of square miles. The problem, of course, is that suburban land looks well tended and intentional, while Detroit's vacant land looks abandoned—overgrown with vegetation, the site of dumped tires and other trash, block after block of ghost streets.

Since all cities spread out following World War II, all cities tend to see gaps in the form of vacant lots deep in the old inner cities. From Philadelphia to Flint to St. Louis to Baltimore, many of these cities report an inventory of vacant lots numbering in the thousands or even tens of thousands. Detroit, from what I can tell from my own travels and observations, and from those of others, probably has more vacant urban land than anywhere else, that is, land once occupied but now slowly returning to nature—close to one hundred thousand vacant residential lots, by one recent survey, plus thousands of former commercial and industrial sites that now stand empty. It's a legacy of all those enormous auto factories that sprang up here a century ago; when they finally fell to the wrecking crews, these vast industrial complexes left huge gaps in Detroit's urban fabric. Then, too, the city's many working-class districts, filled for decades with small wood-frame bungalows and ranches, didn't stand up well to abandonment. If cities like Chicago and Philadelphia, which also saw big population drains to suburbia, still look more urban today than Detroit, it's due at least in part to their inventory of sturdy brick apartment buildings that simply held up better to vacancy that Detroit's bungalows. Youngstown, Ohio, does provide something of a mirror image of Detroit's landscape, with the same rural look of a once-mighty industrial center that lost most of its factories and many of its homes; but Youngstown is barely a fifth of Detroit's geographic size, so its vacancy, while painfully evident, is nothing like the scale of the Motor City's.

That's the bad news. The good news is that almost from the moment people began leaving Detroit and other cities, other people began trying to think of new uses for all that empty space. For a long time, they mostly thought to rebuild on the traditional model, utilizing whatever tax credits and fancy financing they could throw into the breach. Lately, though, as the environmental movement attained greater clout inside cities, as the local food movement took shape, as entrepreneurs began to look at vacant urban land as an asset instead of a liability, the uses suggested for empty urban land began to get more creative. Whole fields of study sprang up on the subject of landscape urbanism. Today, city dwellers plant community gardens on vacant lots, and homeowners in

An abandoned Detroit street in what once was a residential district has been designated for an industrial park but so far remains vacant.

decayed neighborhoods fence in empty lots near their houses to create larger suburban-sized compounds for themselves. Energy-conscious people map ways to construct giant arrays of solar panels on vacant fields in places like Detroit and Youngstown. Agricultural entrepreneurs envision huge farms on previously built-upon city land. Business owners calculate the value of timber harvested from urban reforestation programs. Landscape architects dream of opening up long-buried streams to restore something of the natural landscape paved over so long ago.

Detroit fascinates so many people around the world today in part because the creative possibilities loom greater here than anywhere else. A Michigan State University agriculture study found that Detroiters could grow seventy-five percent of their fruits and vegetables year-round on land within the city (thus reducing dependence on a food chain that brings salad greens to Detroit tables from as far away as Mexico or beyond). Detroit's vacant land, if every inch were covered with solar panels, could generate enough electricity to power every home in the city and many outside it. I mention these estimates not necessarily as realistic possibilities, but to illustrate the scale of Detroit's opportunity. Detroit with its vacant land could not just redevelop itself; it could reimagine what a city ought to be. As a local Detroit activist named Joan Moss said in early 2012, "This is an exciting time to be in the city of Detroit. We almost have a blank slate."

So far, the debate on reusing vacant urban land in Detroit and elsewhere has mostly centered on community gardening, as though agriculture was the default choice if building new homes remains out of the question. But the debate shifts almost daily, and the advocates of solar panels and reforestation and other creative uses gain credence and adherents year by year. Architects and designers have come up with creative solutions to vacant areas long thought beyond help; there's the decommissioned elevated train track in lower Manhattan that became the acclaimed High Line, a fabulously popular greenway, or the overgrown railroad right-of-way in Detroit that stood unused for years until it became the Dequindre Cut, a jogging, strolling, and biking path.

It's hard to keep up with all the new ideas. In this part of this book, we'll survey some of the major ones, assess the potential benefits, and suggest ways to ease these dreams toward fulfillment.

We'll look at the small-scale solutions first.

SIDE LOTS AND SHORT CUTS

As we saw earlier, the Brightmoor neighborhood on Detroit's far west side suffers some of the worst abandonment of any urban district in America. This pervasive vacancy draws all sorts of visitors, many of the vulture type, eager to bag their quota of ruin photographs. But a lot of academic researchers turn up hoping to learn something about how cities react to shrinkage. One of these, Margaret Dewar, a professor of urban planning at the University of Michigan, has studied Brightmoor for several years, working with her students to survey and map the four-square-mile district. Like me she deplores the "ruins voyeurism" and "vacancy tourism" that afflict Detroit today.

Dewar's recent work focuses on what Brightmoor's remaining residents have done to reclaim some of the thousands of vacant lots in their neighborhood. These residents, hardy folk whose parents and grandparents worked in the auto plants nearby and who mostly have lived in Brightmoor for decades, have created a new urban phenomena: They've spread out to take advantage of the vacancy they see all around them. On a block with perhaps just a handful of houses left, the remaining residents often fence in one or more of the vacant lots adjacent to their homes, giving themselves a more suburban-sized lot or compound.

Academics have given this trend various names; a 2008 paper by scholars Tobias Amborst, Daniel D'Oca, and Georgeen Theodore referred to the overall trend as the New Suburbanism and dubbed these larger parcels "blots," a cross between "block" and "lot." I prefer the term "side lot" because I find that more descriptive and easier to grasp. By whatever name, these side lots turn up all over Brightmoor (and elsewhere in Detroit, too.) Dewar and one of her students, Rob Linn, surveyed Brightmoor and counted several hundred of them, with all manner of configurations and all manner of fences surrounding them.

What do homeowners do with their side lots? They plant gardens, store equipment, build additions onto their houses, add a driveway, install play equipment for their kids. Fly over Brightmoor via Google Maps and you may spot swimming pools, new patios, and outbuildings. If family members live nearby, homeowners may fence in two or more lots separating their houses to create a family compound.

To obtain a side lot, some homeowners have gone down to City Hall and slogged through the bureaucracy to legally buy a parcel from the city, which acquired it through tax foreclosure. But often homeowners just fence in the vacant lot next to their home without the blessing of the law. Nearly sixty percent of the side lots studied by Dewar and Linn did not show up in the assessor's records. We may call it squatting, but absent any market demand for the land or meaningful oversight by the city, Dewar and Linn see a lot of good in it: "Their purchase and improvement of property as most property owners disinvested suggested a commitment to the place and a confidence in Brightmoor's future," they write. "Such use of property plays an important role in enabling homeowners to create the environment they want around their homes and to control nearby activities in areas of the city with insufficient police presence."

Dewar and others have noted that by combining two or more of the older, narrower city lots these residents are creating a more suburban feel for themselves. City lots used to measure as little as thirty feet wide, compared to modern suburban lots built to a zoned minimum of one hundred feet wide or larger. And it's not just the acquisition of side lots that can remake a district like Brightmoor. As nonprofit groups like Habitat for Humanity build new houses in Brightmoor, the city's updated zoning dictates that they acquire two of the old narrow lots for each new home built. This, too, produces a more suburbanized landscape over time. Dewar and Linn mapped one block in Brightmoor that showed forty-six distinct lots in 1978; by 2009, the number of lots on that block had shrunk to twenty-seven due to consolidation.

Spend enough time in Brightmoor and you begin to notice other ways the remaining residents reshape their urban landscape. Dewar and Linn counted numerous little footpaths worn into the landscape—short cuts across vacant lots trod over time by local residents. The wider and better traveled of these pedestrian paths sometimes run for blocks parallel to sidewalks or streets, becoming unofficial greenways. More narrow, less traveled ones may lead to a single house. Calling them "tributary" paths, Dewar and Linn note that many link to homes from the rear or side, suggesting that for the most part kids are using them. These paths skirt around occupied homes, illegal dump sites, and other potential obstacles. Some of these unofficial byways show two tracks, indicating that people are using them for vehicles, perhaps to get to and from off-street parking or to avoid detours around impassable roads. This unofficial network of pathways shows Brightmoor residents remaking their urban environment to suit their needs. Visitors often say Brightmoor shows what happens when a neighborhood goes back to nature. But the side lots and short cuts better show what happens when a densely populated urban neighborhood de-densifies and the remaining residents take advantage of it.

It takes place almost entirely without official blessing. As Amborst, D'Oca, and Theodore wrote, "What sets the New Suburbanism apart is the fact that it is gradual, unplanned, uncoordinated, and bottom-up."

As I've said, these side-lot and shortcut uses remain all but invisible to the ruin vultures that come only to gnaw on the bones of the city. Even urban planners attuned to the rhythms of a shrinking city may miss the trend as they scout out the more colorful and better-publicized community gardens. But as Dewar and Linn point out, side lots vie in importance with gardens in the reshaping of Brightmoor. The district now sports dozens of gardens that have been the focus of a good deal of publicity, but there are hundreds of side lots that have drawn little attention. Unimproved vacant lots may still outnumber side lots by a great deal, but side lots provide evidence that a bottom-up reshaping of the urban landscape has been taking place in Brightmoor. "I think if you were looking for change in one year, you'd hardly be able to detect it," Dewar told me. "But over ten years, enormous change, everyday people every day remaking the city." Side lots or no, Brightmoor remains a poor, largely abandoned neighborhood. But clearly not everyone has given up on Brightmoor, and the folks who stick around are reshaping it to their liking as their limited resources permit.

Dewar and Linn offer some common-sense policy prescriptions based on their study. Clearly the city should encourage further investment of this type by residents, since such investment shows a commitment to the neighborhood and a willingness to stay when so many others have fled. Therefore, the city ought to deed property to the homeowners who have taken (officially or not) these side lots; at a minimum, the city could lease the lots to residents at low cost for a long term. And the city could continue to ignore code violations that seem to hurt no one, like violations concerning the height of fences. When the ship is sinking, the skipper ought not criticize what tune the passengers care to whistle.

VACANT LOT RECLAMATIONS

Closely akin to side lots are programs in many cities to reclaim vacant lots with landscaping. Nobody does it better than Philadelphia.

In his younger days, Bob Grossmann worked as an auto worker and a contractor before his love of gardening and his passion for volunteer work drew him to Philadelphia Green, the arm of the venerable Pennsylvania Horticultural Society that plants trees and helps community gardeners. Grossmann runs the society's vacant land restoration program, and in that capacity he has helped develop a model program for rescuing vacant lots in the absence of any market demand for them. Crews hired by Philadelphia Green go to a targeted vacant lot, where they collect the trash, pull the weeds, spread a new layer of topsoil (the old dirt usually being too compromised), plant new grass, perhaps a few trees, and erect a simple post-and-rail fence around the perimeter. These fences have become the trademark of the program, a motif widely imitated elsewhere. Youngstown, for example, models their vacant lot restoration program directly on the Philadelphia Green practice. Under Grossmann's direction, Philadelphia Green has now transformed several thousand vacant lots in the city's poorer neighborhoods. Simply by transforming these lots from trash-strewn eyesores to a small neighborhood amenity, the society added value back to "worthless" land.

Susan Wachter, a professor at the University of Pennsylvania, has studied this program and its impact on local property values. She reported that these vacant-land improvements boosted surrounding home values by as much as thirty percent, which she called "an astonishingly large impact." New tree plantings alone raised housing values about ten percent. Nor do the improvements cost very much. Grossmann told me Philadelphia Green can stabilize a vacant lot—with trash collection, new topsoil, grass, trees, and a fence—for an initial cost of about $1.20 a square foot. For the typical vacant lot, that means the society can transform it for a few thousand dollars, and maintain it all season for a few hundred dollars more. Seldom has an urban recovery effort made its limited dollars go so far.

If greening vacant lots promotes better property values, it also appears to cut down on crime; it even gets nearby residents to exercise more. Those aren't idle boasts, but the meticulously documented findings of a ten-year study conducted by the Perelman School of Medicine at the University of Pennsylvania in Philadelphia. Led by Dr. Charles C. Branas of the Department of Biostatistics and Epidemiology, the study looked at the impact of PHS's greening 4,436 vacant lots in Philadelphia, totaling over 7.8 million square feet, from 1999 to 2008. The study matched the greened lots with control lots that had not been greened, and then used a variety of police statistics and health surveys among residents to measure impacts.

As reported in the *American Journal of Epidemiology*, the study found that greening vacant lots was associated with consistent reductions in gun assaults and other types of crime. Residents living near greened lots reported less stress. Neighbors exercised more.

As always in careful academic studies, the authors refrained from drawing sweeping conclusions, instead suggesting further ideas to study. But it's not hard to see why greening vacant lots on the scale that PHS has can make a difference. As the authors of the study put it:

The "broken windows" theory suggests that vacant lots offer refuge to criminal and other illegal activity and visibly symbolize that a neighborhood has deteriorated, that no one is in control, and that unsafe or criminal behavior is welcome to proceed with little if any supervision. A related theory, the "incivilities" theory, suggests that physical incivilities, such as abandoned vacant lots, promote weak social ties among residents and encourage crimes, ranging from harassment to homicide.

Central to both theories is that criminals are thought to feel emboldened in areas with greater physical disorder while, at the same time, residents are driven toward greater anonymity and are less willing or able to step in and prevent crime. Greening may thus be a partial remedy for disorder.

In terms of specific findings, the analysis showed a significant reduction in gun assaults in all areas studied associated with greening vacant lots. Vandalism and criminal mischief were also significantly reduced after the greening treatment in at least one section of Philadelphia. In terms of health outcomes, vacant lot greening was associated with residents reporting significantly less stress and more exercise.

Just why gun assaults went down is a matter of speculation, but the researchers suggested two plausible reasons. Cleaning up vacant lots discourages crime because the bad guys see that someone in the community is paying attention—it's the opposite of the broken-window effect. Alternatively, weed-choked, garbage-strewn vacant lots may serve as hiding places for illegal firearms or as convenient disposal areas for weapons, and greening the lot deprives the criminals of this haven.

In one odd result, the study found that disorderly conduct actually increased in the presence of greening vacant lots. But the researchers suggested two possible explanations. Either the newly cleaned and attractive lots were drawing bigger (and sometimes disorderly) crowds; or, in the presence of a new neighborhood amenity like a greened lot, tolerance for misbehavior went down and standards of civil behavior rose, resulting in more calls to police *complaining* of disorderly conduct, and more police attention to the problem.

It's not hard to see why the PHS program makes a difference. The scale alone impresses, with PHS, by early 2012, having completed several thousand lot greenings since the late 1990s, with more than ten million dollars invested and more than seventy acres of land in total restored. Nearly two thousand trees have been planted. Moreover, the vacant lot treatments often create dramatic changes in the appearance of any given lot; these changes prove easy to implement; they cost relatively little, especially compared to other, often less successful, urban health and safety programs; and PHS works hand-in-hand with local community residents, building a constituency for the program, instead of the program being imposed as the latest deus ex machina from a distant federal government, state capital, or city hall.

So far, we've looked at the small-scale interventions sized to individual vacant lots or slightly larger. As we turn to urban agriculture, we'll see that growing food inside cities works most often at that same individual lot size. The question to consider later is whether it could work at scales much larger and more ambitious.

Urban Agriculture

As a journalist I've covered urban agriculture for several years, and the more I learn about growing food inside cities, the less I believe it's about *food*. Enthusiasts for the urban agriculture movement try to build communities, using small plots of land as rallying points. They bring people together at these gardens to celebrate their neighborhoods, to clean up a blighted vacant lot, to dispel drug dealers from the street corner, to welcome immigrants to America, or to shelter battered women within a productive enterprise. The food produced seems almost incidental, except in a few large, well-organized gardens like Earthworks and D-Town Farm in Detroit or Spring Gardens in Philadelphia. As a saying has it, community gardening is more about *community* than *gardening*.

That's not to say that gardeners don't grow a lot of food in places like Detroit, where the nonprofit Greening of Detroit organization counts more than twelve hundred family, school, and community gardens in the city. Most of these—the vast majority—remain tiny, often measuring no more than one vacant house lot or even smaller. Estimates of how much food gets grown on these plots seem to me to be mostly guesswork, like the Greening of Detroit's estimate from 2009 of 330,000 pounds of food produced that year in Detroit. But the presence of hope is real, and spirit remains the best fertilizer. If growers bring the proper enthusiasm and get the right technical help, even Detroit dirt can prove amazingly productive, as it does at the nonprofit Earthworks farm on the city's east side, where dozens of crops go to feed the needy at the nearby Capuchin Soup Kitchen. Of course, some local growers bring less skill, or less commitment, than others to their patch of green. Sometimes you can visit a small urban garden in the fall and see tomatoes or lettuce that nobody has picked wasting away. Nor is urban agriculture a moneymaker in any real sense yet. Whatever revenue local growers raise at the Grown in Detroit table at Eastern Market or other markets in the city, it's no more than a sliver of the revenue raised by fast food outlets in the city, let alone the billions of dollars spent each year by Detroiters on food.

Having said this much, I believe that urban agriculture *could* grow into something much bigger, producing much more food and much more revenue—provided that cities and their people accept scaled-up urban farming as one solution to the opportunity presented by so much vacant land. It's not at all clear in Detroit that the city and its people embrace that idea. In mid-2009, interviewing east-side Detroiters about renovation efforts, I listened to one longtime resident named Sandra Butler say, "I don't want farmland. I just want homes. I just don't want, when I'm driving down these streets, seeing corn and beans. I just don't want to see that." Another Detroit woman, Sheryl Bolden, echoed that: "I see enough pheasants and all of that. I don't need no more."

Certainly the City of Detroit has for years (as of mid-2012) delayed approval of proposals like Hantz Farms and Recovery Park, two suggestions for large-scale commercial farming that we'll look at a little later. City officials repeatedly cite Michigan's Right to Farm law as one reason; the law protects farmers from regulatory interference and lawsuits as new suburbs spring up nearby, and city officials fear commercial growers could use the law to escape any meaningful regulation. But mostly it comes down to a political choice, and city leaders, so far, have not embraced urban agriculture (or, for that matter, any other large-scale unconventional use) as a long-term interim use for Detroit's vast tracts of urban prairie.

So the topic of urban agriculture neatly splits into two categories—the success stories of the nonprofit community gardeners, and the potential success stories inherent in scaled-up commercial growing as a tool of economic development in post-industrial cities. Both bear closer examination if we're to understand the positions of our cities today.

We'll start with the community gardeners.

Riet Schumack, Brightmoor

Born in Holland six decades ago, Riet Schumack was a young woman when she met an American engineer, fell in love, married, and came to the United States to start a new life. That life was comfortable by any middle-class standard. Her husband was a professor at the University of Detroit Mercy, and the family lived in Detroit's Rosedale Park neighborhood, a district filled with brick Tudors and other sturdy residences. But Riet was not the type to just settle in, and over time, her devotion to her Christian faith led to membership in the activist Christian Community Development Association, which urged its members to follow the Three *r*'s: relocation, redistribution, and reconciliation. "So in order to be effective," Riet explains, "you *relocate*"—that is, you leave your comfortable home and move into the poorer district you wish to help; there you *redistribute* ("not just money, but whatever talents you have and who you are and just sharing your personality with your neighbors"), and thus achieve a *reconciliation* with those you might have ignored in a previous lifestyle. And as if to put this rugged faith to its ultimate test, Riet chose to practice the three *r*'s in what arguably qualifies as America's most abandoned urban village, the Detroit neighborhood of Brightmoor.

We've visited Brightmoor before in this book, and a reader will recall the shoddy shacks put up in the 1920s for a clientele from Appalachia and the Deep South, structures mostly swept away by now, to be replaced by, well, by nothing, except the tall grasses and piles of dumped tires and other trash. About twelve thousand people called Brightmoor home as of the 2010 census, and most were long-term residents who remain clannish toward newcomers, even well-meaning ones like Riet. "The people here are survivors," Riet told me in 2011. "They took care of themselves, and they still do. They are fiercely independent." They also, she added, take a good long time to trust any new entry on the block. "We moved here in 2006, and it was not until 2010 that doors were open and people were open to relationships and so on," she said. "So it took three to four years to gain trust, but once you gain that trust, they were go-getters, they were."

Riet brought two enthusiasms with her—gardening and children—and set to work among her newfound friends to meld both interests in some way. She started a youth garden and invited kids from the neighborhood to come and grow vegetables. The high-school dropout rate in the neighborhood is more than fifty percent, and Riet was hoping that by building relationships with the kids more of them would stay in school.

It didn't work too well at first; the kids seemed mostly bored with gardening, and efforts to freshen it up for them by creating art projects didn't work, either. Soon, though, Riet and a few other neighbors were giving kids a real say in what to grow, and they encouraged them to sell the produce at local farmers' stands and keep whatever money they made. They taught the kids to process the vegetables in various ways, developing a few job skills and perhaps some life skills along the way.

Riet learned at a Greening of Detroit class that community gardens often deter crime, so she tested that thesis by creating her first community garden near a drug house. "And, boy, was it ever right," she says. "Probably within six weeks the drug house was closed down and we had this big cowboy to-do, you know, dogs and police, it was very fun. We used to have prostitutes rotating in our street all the time and drug dealing—it all stopped. Once the children started playing in the gardens and people were out in the street, you know, the drug dealers don't feel comfortable."

There's a lot of old stock yet in Brightmoor, people who have always lived there or the children and grandchildren of the district's original residents, and many had stayed more or less behind locked doors for years. Now the doors started opening and neighbors started coming together again.

"People started gardens," Riet says. "First family gardens, then another community garden across the street, then we started another garden, then little by little it increased, and then we actually had some people moving into the neighborhood. So it was little by little, but then last year [2010] it was like everything exploded. People really took notice and everybody wanted gardens." Brightmoor now sports an edible playscape, a bird garden, a butterfly garden—a few dozen in all, just within a fourteen-block section that was among the hardest hit by abandonment. "Everybody wanted to be part of this because it is so exciting," Riet says.

Materials—wood, paint, seeds for the gardens—are either secondhand or donated. Occasionally Riet gets a small grant, say, a thousand dollars to build raised beds in a garden—wooden boxes in which fruits and vegetables grow in fresh dirt because the Brightmoor soil is too compromised in places. Riet sometimes motors around the neighborhood on a small red tractor, mowing vacant lots and the like. She helped popularize a neighborhood rule that anyone who comes up with a good suggestion for a new type of garden must be willing to work on it personally, albeit with help and donations from others. And she espouses a positive attitude as a key weapon against the poverty and despair all around them.

"In our meetings, we are not allowed to whine," Riet says. "As soon as somebody starts complaining, everybody jumps on him and says, 'No whining!' We all know it's bad. We all know there is no money, it's no use talking about that, let's be creative and let's find out what we can do to make this place better."

A neighborhood man named Craig illustrates the sort of good all this does. Craig was in his early fifties, a native of Brightmoor, out of work, grumpy and nasty, but he did work his own small family garden. So one day Riet left him a flyer from her garden resource group. "Little by little he started coming to activities," she recalled. Riet suggested Craig start selling his vegetables at one of the Greening of Detroit's market tables at the farmers' markets, and in one month he earned something like six hundred dollars. "Boy, that piqued his interest like, 'Oh, I can do this, this is good,'" Riet said. He later got a job with Greening of Detroit. "In 2010, he had become a completely different man," Riet said. "He was smiling, he does volunteer work. He comes to all the meetings. He planted another orchard. He doubled his garden. So to me, this is what it is all about."

It would amount to a wild exaggeration to say that community gardening has reversed decades of blight in Brightmoor. Poverty there remains among the worst in the city, and vacancy grows by the week. But neither can anyone claim the gardeners have wasted their time. Community gardening (remember, it's more about *community* than *gardening*) has brought a spirit back to this distressed urban enclave. True, in some of these neighborhoods it may seem more of a *rural* spirit than an *urban* one. At the popular D-Town Farm elsewhere on Detroit's west side, we find Detroit's biggest community garden at four acres and growing, conceived and run by the charismatic Malik Yakini of the Detroit Black Community Food Security Network; on a warm late-summer Saturday, hundreds of neighbors pick vegetables, buy produce at the farm stand, dance to a live band, and otherwise enjoy the easy, bucolic way of life. There's not a tall building in sight.

I prefer, though, to think of Brightmoor and places like it not so much as an emptying city returning to nature than as a hybrid model of post-industrial urbanism. It blends life off the grid with the limited urban services available in a distressed city. Riet Schumack thinks Brightmoor represents not a failure but a winning strategy for the future.

> I firmly believe in the peak oil phenomenon. I think we have had our cake, we cannot eat it. From here on out our energy is going to become more and more expensive, and we have to deal with it. Our children are not going to live the same way that we did. They are going to have to live on a lot less energy, food prices are going to go up, and transportation prices are going to go up, and housing prices are going to go up. So, I think Brightmoor is perfectly positioned to meet that challenge. We can reinvent this neighborhood any way we want. I think that's a beautiful place to start to build a sustainable society.

Spring Gardens, Philadelphia

I think of all the community gardens I've seen, in city after city, my favorite is Philadelphia's Spring Gardens. Nestled in a near north side district a ten-minute walk from downtown skyscrapers, the garden neatly tucks into a two-acre square block framed on three sides by brick townhouses. A tall iron ornamental fence surrounds the garden; artwork and community meeting tables and tents occupy the middle ground; to either side, nearly two hundred individual plots unfurl in lush symmetry. America's community gardening movement accomplishes a great many things, from assimilating immigrants to feeding poor people to providing a venue for artists, but Spring Gardens ranks among the few that do all of that at the same time. Perhaps none do it all so well.

Stephen White, a local architect who lives in the neighborhood, helped found Spring Gardens back in the mid-1990s, when the district was heading in the wrong direction, with rising rates of vacancy, crime, and poverty. Tall and lean,

Stephen White, one of the founders of the Spring Gardens community farming project in Philadel-phia, delights in showing visitors around. (Author photo)

wearing an ancient sun hat, White told me during one of my visits how this square block had just six houses left on it in 1995 instead of the forty or so that it once held, and people were living in just three of the remaining structures. White and his fellow neighborhood activists prevailed on the city to relocate the remaining residents and clear the block for a garden.

"One of our hopes was that it would do something to unify our neighborhood," White told me. "Our neighborhood was divided between the east half and the west half, sort of the white-collar workers, the blue-collar workers, the haves and have-nots, all kind of differences."

As White strolled through the garden with me in the fall of 2011, introducing me to some of the gardeners and explaining the features, he talked about the transformation: "When we started the garden, people from both parts of the neighborhood came to work together, rolled up their sleeves, and it just kind of turned into a unity or harmony of people that understood each other better, and the miracles spread. That was the beginning of a rebirth of this neighborhood."

It took plenty of hard work. When contractors razed houses on the block, they did what urban demolition contractors often do, dumping the debris right into the basements, covering it with the thinnest possible smear of dirt. So the neighbors first had to haul away a lot of the broken concrete and doors and all kinds of junk; they formed what amounted to a six-foot berm surrounding the entire block, finally persuading the city's redevelopment office to take it away. The quality of the remaining dirt was pretty poor, as urban dirt often is, so the gardeners built their raised beds—boxes filled with a good mix of fresh dirt from afar—and they began to grow.

In the early days, drug dealing still took place nearby, and thieves stole a lot of stuff, but eventually the gardeners got funding through the local community development group to build a fence. They kept begging until they had enough money to build a really good fence, the centerpiece of which is a beautiful iron gate whose curlicues created Spring Gardens' marketing image, an artistic motif that appears on its T-shirts.

At first gardeners grew annuals and a few vegetables, but as families moved back into the neighborhood and interest in the garden grew, the output grew more effusive. About 175 families now tend plots at Spring Gardens. A committee chooses growers from a waiting list. The number varies a little year by year as some growers want larger or smaller plots. The biggest single section is a twenty-by-forty-foot plot reserved for the City Harvest program, part of a program that sees prisoners in the local corrections system grow seedlings that are then transferred to dozens of gardens through the city, including this one. The food from that effort goes to the Share Food Network, which helps distressed families get the nutrition they need along with food counseling and cooking demonstrations. Spring Gardens alone produces about fifteen hundred pounds of food each year for the network from its plot, and citywide the dozens of gardeners participating have delivered more than 130,000 pounds of food to families over a six-year span. "It's their only source of fresh food, and on top of that it's organic and really fresh and just terrific," White told me.

Spring Gardens' watering system takes advantage of a nearby fire hydrant. A two-inch pipe winds throughout the two-acre site, and each day in season volunteers open faucets at various points along this pipe to fill up large plastic drums, from which growers draw what they need.

(An aside: Post-industrial cities take for granted their abundant supply of fresh water, never reflecting, except in a vague sort of way, on the scarcity of water elsewhere. Yet water remains critical to these cities' history, and, as we saw earlier, it may help create their future, too. All these places sprouted because of access to water, both for manufacturing uses and for transportation. Think of St. Louis on the Mississippi, Detroit on its strait (*detroit*), Pittsburgh on its three rivers, Cleveland where the Cuyahoga meets Lake Erie, Buffalo where Erie funnels into the Niagara. The water that gurgles through the pipe at Spring Gardens would, in some parts of the world, be as valuable as the food itself.)

Spring Gardens today retains its rich mix of urban yuppies, seniors, and Mexican and Puerto Rican immigrant growers. During one of my tours, White stopped to show me one plot tended by a Puerto Rican family, pointing out that the immigrant growers typically make the plots into almost mini-farms, growing as much as possible—beans in the spring, peppers later in the season. Nearby, a Mexican woman and her two girls were tending their potatoes, peppers, raspberries, and tomatoes. For some gardeners, the farming provides an outlet for city stress, a chance for office workers to get their hands dirty growing flowers they can cut and take home, or perhaps just a place to sit in the sun. "So we have just literally all kinds of gardeners, and we have all kinds of backgrounds," White told me. "We have our annual picnics in summer, and in the fall we have delicious meals of various kinds, and it's pretty exciting. We have residents from the medical schools, we have all kinds of professions, young people, people with just a couple of little kids, and their primary thing is to raise their children so that they know that the food doesn't just come wrapped in plastic."

Community gardens in Philadelphia, like those in Detroit, Milwaukee, and elsewhere, benefit from a network of support, like the Pennsylvania Horticultural Society's Community Growers Alliance in Philadelphia and the Greening of Detroit in the Motor City. These organizations help get growers started with seeds and seedlings, mulch, compost, tools, and instruction to provide the know-how. The parent organizations in turn get their support from foundations and other donors. Even the tiniest garden plot usually flourishes as part of a much larger network.

By now, academic researchers have begun to publish findings showing that places like Spring Gardens tend to bolster property values in their neighborhoods. White provides some anecdotal evidence for that. "Right across the street, some of these houses were worth on order of forty thousand dollars before the garden started," he told me. "Now you wouldn't get one for less than a half a million."

COMMERCIAL FARMING INSIDE CITIES

We could multiply our examples of community gardens, visiting Growing Power in Milwaukee (run by the charismatic MacArthur fellow Will Allen) and the amazingly productive Earthworks Urban Farm in Detroit, where a bounty of food goes to feed the needy at the nearby Capuchin Soup Kitchen. But it's time to ask whether larger-scale commercial farming, as opposed to the community gardens we've just looked at, has any place in the future of our cities.

All of the community gardens we see around the country share certain traits—they're small, nonprofit, run by volunteers, funded by donations, with the food either consumed by the growers, given away free to neighbors, or donated to community food banks. The largest of the community gardens I've visited— D-Town Farm on Detroit's west side—occupies about four acres of open land; most community gardens operate at smaller scales. Even the most impressive rarely measure more than the two-acre size of Spring Gardens and Earthworks; the vast majority, like the edible playscapes and butterfly gardens that Riet Schumack and her neighbors have created in Brightmoor, often measure just a small fraction of an acre. I myself have grown and eaten tomatoes and carrots from a neighborhood garden in Detroit measuring no more than about thirty by thirty feet, or roughly two percent of an acre. My personal observation tells me that that size remains typical of community gardens.

If community gardening does so much good—and it does an enormous amount of good by uniting neighborhoods, feeding the poor, and bolstering property values—then why even consider scaling it up to commercial size? Because all of our post-industrial cities share a dire need for jobs and tax base and new uses for vacant urban land. Farming presents one way to achieve that. Most of the real money in farming comes in the processing of the food, and Detroit and other industrial cities with an abundance of manufacturing sites and a history of making things would take naturally to food processing. And as the world grows hotter and drier, as good agricultural land in California and other places disappears in the face of drought or new development, cities may want (indeed, they may need) to source more of their food locally. Urban agriculture on a large scale provides one way to do that.

But proposals for large-scale urban agriculture in Detroit and other cities prompt a host of questions. Who would work these farms, and how do we create a food network, an infrastructure, to get the produce to market when no such network exists now inside cities? How to tax urban agricultural land? How to deal with livestock nuisances and truck traffic in residential neighborhoods, and how to protect the community gardeners from competition by commercial farming?

These are complex questions, and even in my enthusiasm for an experiment of trying commercial farming inside cities, I would not predict an easy path ahead. To put it bluntly, large-scale farming inside cites may not work. The profit margins would be thin, the labor often unpleasant, the urban workforce mostly untrained, the organizational infrastructure nonexistent.

Nonetheless, I believe that several benefits suggest themselves. Commercial farming creates jobs, and Detroit and all other post-industrial cities hunger for jobs as much as for food itself. Commercial farming could put vacant surplus urban land back into productive use, land that otherwise will continue to sit empty and untaxed, a drag on city services and budgets for years to come. And commercial farming takes us down the road toward reimagining our cities, thinking of new uses for buildings that once hummed with factory production and land that once thrived as working-class and middle-class neighborhoods. Absent better ideas—and Detroit and other post-industrial cities are starved for useful ideas right now—commercial farming inside cities rates at least a tryout.

Recovery Park

Gary Wozniak grew up in Detroit's northern suburbs when roads that later became major highways were still two-lane byways for a few miles beyond city limits and dirt roads after that. His grandparents owned a fifty-acre truck farm, and young Gary would help them sell their vegetables on weekly expeditions to Detroit's Eastern Market and other farmers' markets in the area. Later, in the 1980s, Wozniak became a stockbroker, and in the go-go atmosphere of those years he got in trouble, as many others did, by abusing first cocaine and then his clients' money. He spent three and a half years in a federal prison in Duluth, MN, got into recovery, straightened out his life, and formed a lasting bond with the people at a Detroit agency called SHAR, for Self-Help Addiction Rehabilitation.

In the next couple of decades, while staying clean, Wozniak owned several restaurants, a mortgage company, ran a health club, did financial planning, and otherwise used his financial skills. When the Great Recession hit, he sold the last of his companies and accepted SHAR's invitation to join the organization as a consultant. Leaders of the nonprofit agency wanted Wozniak to help them straighten out their finances, which were perilous, and over the summer and early fall of 2008 he worked with them to re-organize their operation. But cash flow remained the big problem. Subsidies for treating some of the two thousand or so addicts and returning prisoners that SHAR saw each year did not cover the cost of the operation. Wozniak began toying with the idea of starting a social enterprise, a commercial activity run for nonprofit ends. One day that October he

Gary Wozniak, the one-time stockbroker turned urban-farming enthusiast, on the eastside Detroit site he hopes to turn into a demonstration project. (Author photo)

tossed out the idea of urban agriculture. The SHAR directors said yes almost at once and gave him ten thousand dollars in seed money to figure it all out. At that point, of course, there was no site for a farm, no employees, no business plan, nothing but a vague idea.

"I know really well what can happen with an addiction," Wozniak told me in late 2011. "I know that there is an answer, when you stop using, how to rebuild your life. I've been fortunate that I've got skills developed over a lifetime to be able to look at business ideas and handle money. I want to use those development skills to really help the recovery community rebuild the city."

Urban agriculture appealed to his business sense. More than anything, SHAR's clients needed jobs. As addicts and returning prisoners—often illiterate and lacking any job skills or career history—they were incapable even of most auto factory jobs, which today require computer skills and probably a couple of years of college. Agriculture, though, still hires lots of low-skilled and semi-skilled workers; indeed, farming can hardly get along without such workers. Farming, Wozniak reasoned, could provide not just a paycheck for SHAR's clients but some life-management skills, too, like how to show up on time every day and how to understand instructions and get along with co-workers and bosses. And, he likes to say, the plants don't care if the person tending to them can read or write.

What evolved over the next year or two was a plan to create a large farm employing SHAR clients on vacant land that once was the site of Detroit's Northeastern High School, demolished many years ago. That site by itself would provide twenty acres or so, and with other vacant parcels nearby Wozniak figured he could put together about sixty acres, and expand his model elsewhere as opportunity arose. He wasn't thinking of planting just once a year, as most community gardeners do in Detroit and other cities. He wanted year-round production, the better to keep revenue flowing, so he mapped a plan to use hoop houses—long narrow plastic-wrapped tents or huts stretched over a metal framework—which allow growing even in winter. Processing the food—tomatoes into salsa, and the like—would take place nearby in a refitted industrial building. At another factory site in the city, he would install fiberglass tanks to raise tilapia fish, the fiberglass tanks fabricated at still another Detroit site.

Visit with Wozniak a while and you hear as much about revenue streams and production schedules as you do about addiction and recovery.

But his Recovery Park grew even beyond that. Wozniak met with hundreds of community residents, ministers, local business owners, and other constituencies—anyone who might conceivably touch or be touched by his plans—and he evolved a plan that included playgrounds, new housing, recreational corridors, all knitted together with his farming operation. At its most expansive, Recovery Park would spread out over two thousand acres of Detroit's east side, or about three square miles. And it would employ hundreds of people, nearly all of them Detroiters who otherwise would earn nothing due to their low skills.

So far, so good. Throughout this period—say, 2009 through 2011—Wozniak was also speaking with Detroit's city council members, their staffs, city workers in Planning and Development, state workers in Lansing. He briefed Detroit mayor Dave Bing and Michigan governor Rick Snyder on his plans. He got lots of positive feedback. What he didn't get was a go-ahead from the City of Detroit.

Detroit, like other post-industrial cities, lacks any zoning ordinance for farming activities. That doesn't stop the numerous community gardeners from working their small plots, but it does get in the way of the sort of major operation Wozniak envisioned. The City Planning Commission, an advisory arm to city council, began the tedious process of considering all the many legal issues involved with a zoning change. The very notion of farming inside a city frightened a lot of people, from the neighbors who didn't want to smell manure or awake to roosters to city planners who harbored doubts about their ability to control and regulate urban agriculture once they set it loose. Wozniak had hoped he'd plant crops in spring of 2010 at the latest; then in spring of 2011; and in early 2012 he still wasn't sure whether another year would go by before he'd be allowed to show what Recovery Park could do for the city.

What no one seemed to realize is how little land Recovery Park needed to start a demonstration plot and create its first few dozen jobs. Even if Recovery Park took a hundred acres of Detroit dirt, it would amount to the tiniest sliver of the city's many thousands of acres of vacant land; and it would be no more than a single drop of water in the sea of Michigan's statewide agriculture, estimated to cover millions of acres.

"The city needs some wins," Wozniak told me in late 2011. "Agriculture, food-system development are quick wins. There are a number of projects, not just Recovery Park that can happen relatively quickly that can bring jobs. It can bring revenue. It can solidify some neighborhoods. And I really think we need to move ahead with it." He continued:

> Even if farming is intermediate, try it. If it's successful and if it attracts people back into the community, then you can transition to a permanent use. If it doesn't work, at least you've got some cleaned-up land, and you can look at another option for it. But just letting it sit there when it costs the city to mow it and maintain it and keep the infrastructure just doesn't make sense to me. It's frustrating. You would think that with all the land that we have available, we have all this need for low-tech job development, bringing jobs to the workforce, that that would have really opened up the floodgates a lot quicker than it has.

His experience mirrored that of businessman John Hantz, a Detroiter who sparked the city's debate on large-scale farming in early 2009 by proposing Hantz Farms, his vision for a two-thousand-acre operation that he planned to bankroll himself from his profits as a financial services businessman on land that he hoped to get from the city. Hantz ran into the same public skepticism, the same downsizing of the plan from two thousand acres to one hundred to something even smaller, the same delays. Eventually in 2011, city council agreed to sell his Hantz Farms operation just three acres of vacant city-owned property near a warehouse Hantz owned on Detroit's east side. But Council barred him from planting any crops on it or selling anything he grew there. He and his Hantz Farms president, a former Michigan State University agriculture extension counselor named Mike Score, would be allowed only to clean up the blighted lots and landscape them. In late 2011, they planted several hundred hardwood saplings there, each a couple of feet tall, with the expectation that by the time they matured, city council would have finally blessed Hantz's larger farming project. By mid-2012, the Bing administration said it was ready to sell another 175 acres to Hantz for tree-planting, a major advance of the project; but planners at City Council were already reacting skeptically, and as I write this in summer 2012 it remains unclear what's ahead for the project.

Riet Schumach and her red tractor are a familiar site in Detroit's Brightmoor neighborhood. (Author photo)

Wozniak acknowledges that Detroit's fiscal crisis, the jailing of former mayor Kwame Kilpatrick, the national real-estate bust, and the credit crunch all conspired to draw attention away from the approval process for Recovery Park and Hantz Farms. Even so, for an entrepreneur used to living by his wits, the delays stung. "If I wasn't working with a nonprofit, and if I was a for-profit guy, going back to my old world, I would have pulled out a year and a half, two years ago," Wozniak said.

But Wozniak is more the happy warrior than the sorehead. In early 2012, while still awaiting city approval, Recovery Park received a one-million-dollar funding commitment from the Erb Foundation to continue planning and development of the concept—a major boost. Wozniak remains the optimist, and convinced that Recovery Park will indeed flourish and create new jobs and tax revenue for the city. After all, he knows that daily miracles really do happen in the lives of people, and perhaps in the lives of cities, too.

Park Supermarket in Holland

Detroiters, of course, aren't the only people looking to large-scale agriculture as one possible future for cities. Projects are dotting the globe, even if most, like Recovery Park and Hantz Farms, remain mostly in the planning or prototype stage. One potential large-scale project getting a lot of attention for its innovative use of technology is the Park Supermarket near Rotterdam, Holland. Developed by the Rotterdam-based architectural firm Van Bergen Kolpa Architects, the project, still in planning as of early 2012, would fill up a four-thousand-acre plot of scrubland in Randstad, Holland's largest metropolitan area that skirts the fringes of Rotterdam and The Hague. The potential customer base of Park Supermarket exceeds one million people.

Holland enjoys a relatively mild climate, but the goal of the project, as lead architect Jago van Bergen told me in a phone call in late 2011, is to make it milder still within the confines of the farm—creating a more Mediterranean or even tropical clime with a longer growing season and, thus, the ability to produce fruits, vegetables, and grains as diverse as, for example, kiwi and Arborio rice.

Part of the impetus for the project derives from dissatisfaction with urban sprawl. Cities in Holland retain a lot of agricultural land around them, but as those cities spread out, the farmland is getting gobbled up. Civic leaders would like to encourage urban agriculture sites to serve multiple uses: as urban oases, as recreational venues, and as demonstration areas for green technology.

"The cities surrounding the proposed site are home to 170 different eating cultures—from Moroccan to Indonesian, from Turkish to Chinese— and we're aiming to grow food to satisfy all their tastes," van Bergen told one interviewer. "The plan is to divide the park into three climate zones—moderate, Mediterranean, and tropical. Because this will also be a recreational space, our goal is to make it as open as possible, without using greenhouses."

Van Bergen told me local officials commissioned the project both to improve the economic efficiency of local farms and to forge a more sustainable link between food production and city dwellers. "You could also imagine that the people in the city go on a bike ride for the weekends and go there for recreation and come back with some nice produce," he said.

Achieving that requires an array of innovations, some of which are updates of ancient techniques. One type is known as "snake walls"—undulating walls made from clay that curve over crops to shield them from cold winds, as well as storing the heat of the day, a method long used in vineyards to help grapes achieve maturity. Then there are more futuristic "climate pylons," towers that emit clouds of water mist that help to hold warm air at ground level instead of letting it dissipate.

For more tropical items like mangoes, van Bergen said the project would rely on geothermal wells—pipes sunk deep underground to tap the natural heating and cooling qualities of the earth. He noted that we already use geothermal wells for many things, from heating and cooling "green" buildings to helping keep soccer pitches from freezing, so it's not that much of a stretch.

Mostly the project would achieve a more sustainable output simply by growing food so close to customers in cities. Modern agriculture requires a huge amount of fossil fuel for use in fertilizers, in the processing of food, and in the delivery of food across hundreds or thousands of miles. In the pithy phrase of environmentalist and author Bill McKibben, almost everything we eat comes marinated in oil—crude oil. Park Supermarket would cut down on that by giving city dwellers kiwis grown near at hand instead of imported from New Zealand, or farm-raised tilapia fish just a short hop from tank to table.

Critics have questioned whether creating microclimates like this might prove more boondoggle than boon. Dr. Nicola Canon, a lecturer in crop sciences at the Royal Agricultural College in England, told an interviewer that she worries about creating artificial climates in an age of global warming, and that extending the growing season may also give pests and diseases more room to flourish. And she also wondered whether Park Supermarket, like other "green" demonstration projects, might suck up more energy than it saves.

"In my experience, it takes a lot of resources to create a relatively small microclimate," she said. "This means land that could otherwise be used for growing native crops is taken up with technology—whether it be rows and rows of snake walls or climate pylons or whatever."

Despite such doubts, Park Supermarket was winning international kudos in 2011 and 2012, and van Bergen was looking forward to a demonstration project soon.

If nothing else, Park Supermarket, Hantz Farms, Recovery Park, and similar projects illustrate the imagination focused now on growing large amounts of food inside cities. Clearly our cities should allow projects like these to show what they can do. If they fail, our cities are no worse off; and if they succeed, we will have created productive new uses for urban land. "It's very much about the open areas," van Bergen told me. "It can revitalize communities in a very good way."

RESTORING THE NATURAL LANDSCAPE

Steve Vogel grew up on a farm in Indiana in the 1950s, and like many a farm boy, he heard the call of the big city. As a student in the architecture school at the University of Detroit in the '60s, he got involved in affordable-housing work, rehabbing homes in the city, and after graduation in 1970 he worked with nonprofit neighborhood groups to put together housing projects. A few years later, he and two partners founded an architectural firm, Schervish Vogel Merz, and their first contract called on them to map out, and later to design, a series of linked waterfront parks along the City of Detroit's east riverfront. The work earned Vogel and his partners a reputation for adaptive reuse of historic buildings (the firm itself worked out of a converted carriage house on the city's near-east side), as well as landscape architecture and waterfront design.

Working on the parks project, Vogel learned a lot about Detroit's complex network of underground sewer lines. Like many cities, Detroit's sewers carried both sewage and, during heavy rains, rainwater overflow that sometimes bypasses the treatment plant to empty directly into the Detroit River. Once, on "kill day" at Eastern Market, when slaughterhouses were at work, Vogel was standing on the riverbank when he saw the carcass of a pig float by, having been dumped into a sewer. "That was the sort of situation at that time," he told me in late 2011.

One of Detroit's underground sewer lines in particular intrigued Vogel. The city called it Bloody Run after the traditional name of a stream that had, a century or so before, been encased in culverts and turned into a conduit for sewage. The term Bloody Run replaced the name the French had given to this stream (Parents Creek) after an incident in 1763, when Chief Pontiac's Ottawa braves surprised and nearly massacred a contingent of British soldiers near the creek, turning its waters red. Detroiters, like residents in virtually all other cities, used their natural streams as dumping grounds for all manner of refuse and sewage; cholera epidemics that swept the city led to demands for reform. The result: Bloody Run and Detroit's other streams (like urban streams the world over) disappeared underground, turned into sewer lines, buried, and paved over.

"Now the reason this creek interested us was that when we were designing these parks we wanted to have different scales of water," Vogel told me. "The Detroit River, which is so beautiful, is a large scale. We wanted to have smaller scales of water in the park." In the city's waterfront Chene Park, which was the first one they did, Vogel and his partners created a small pond, still there today, and tried to think of ways to bring the water up a few blocks to Jefferson Avenue, one of the city's main streets that parallels the riverfront. "We thought by taking water north up to Jefferson, we could connect the park system better into the city, that people driving down Jefferson could have a visual relationship to the waterfront," he said. If you drive down Jefferson today, he noted, you are not aware of the riverfront. You can't really see it that well in most spots. That led Vogel to the idea of what would happen if you took Bloody Run Creek out of the sewer and actually opened it up and brought it to the park system on the riverfront.

"Daylighting" is the term for opening up a long-buried stream and restoring it to something like its natural state. We can never fully restore the natural state that the first Europeans found. In the name of progress we have done too much over the decades to our landscape—imported invasive flora, polluted too much of our waterways, filled in too many hollows, and bulldozed too many hillsides. But even as Vogel was thinking about getting Bloody Run out from underground again, many cities the world over had begun to try, at least in some fashion, to restore some of what nature begat.

The first reason is easy—money. We taxpayers pay a lot (hundreds of millions of dollars or more in a big city) to create monster-sized sewage treatment plants, and part of what those plants process is just rainwater running off our parking lots and streets into the sewers. The storm water sloshes around with the bad stuff and, on really heavy rain days, overflows onto beaches and into creeks and streams. By daylighting streams, we restore some of nature's natural sponging ability to manage heavy rains; it runs off into streams or soaks into nearby floodplains, giving all that rainwater runoff some place to go besides the sewers. Indeed, a natural landscape absorbs rainwater in many ways, from droplets that stay on the leaves of trees or get drawn up into the roots to creeks that swell in a heavy rain and carry it away.

But saving money is hardly the only motive. The real backers of daylighting come from the ranks of environmentalists, urban pioneers, and community activists. One such individual, Shaun Nethercott, founder and executive director of the environmentally minded Matrix Theatre in Detroit, told me in 2010 that daylighting Bloody Run would be one way for Detroit to reestablish a healthy connection with the natural world.

"It creates a cooling effect, literally a living air conditioner for the city, and makes a softer, greener, cooler landscape," she said. "Being in a green environment reduces anxiety, builds a sense of place, reduces all kinds of symptoms. We need to be connected to a whole life-giving environment, and this is a real way to do it."

Daylighting has gotten a lot of attention around the world in recent years. The city of Seoul, South Korea, went so far as to rip out a downtown expressway to restore the Cheonggyecheon, the city's "pristine stream," in a project hailed internationally; the visionary mayor who headed the project, Lee Myung-Bak, rode his popularity into the presidency of South Korea. Kalamazoo, three hours to the west of Detroit, daylighted its long-buried Arcadia Creek in the 1990s, creating a new downtown waterfront amenity, sparking real-estate development along its route, and helping solve the problem of wet basements in downtown buildings. California has a dozen or more daylighting projects in some stage.

In Detroit, the idea of daylighting Bloody Run became one of the motifs of Steve Vogel's forty-year career. He and his partners suggested it early on to city officials, getting an enthusiastic reception but no money to make it happen. Later, working with the famed activist Grace Lee Boggs, Vogel mapped out a daylighted Bloody Run as part of a Utopian plan known as Adamah, a Hebrew word meaning "of the earth," in which the stream would have created the core of a nonprofit, self-sustaining community of mutually supportive Detroiters. There were other variations as well, all of which died due to the lack of money and the complexity of restoring a stream with a three-thousand-acre watershed in the midst of a major city.

Then, one day, a University of Detroit Mercy alum and former Detroiter named Richard Baron visited Vogel in his office. Baron had built himself a career as one of the nation's most prolific developers of urban residential projects coast to coast. Vogel's firm had done some master planning work for one of Baron's developments. Baron saw some of the Bloody Run sketches on a table and asked about them.

"We said, 'Well, it's not a real project,'" Vogel recalled. "'This is a project we made up and we have no client.' So he said, 'Well, that's a really interesting idea.'" That was it for the time being. Years went by. Then one day Baron called Vogel from the Kresge Foundation, a nonprofit based in suburban Detroit that is a leader in promoting environmentally sensitive work. Baron was looking for a project to do in his native city, remembered the Bloody Run idea, and had gotten the Kresge folks intrigued. So after more talks, the Kresge Foundation gave Vogel, then the dean of architecture at UDM, a grant of five hundred thousand dollars to really work on the idea of daylighting Bloody Run. Baron hoped to bring some other funding along to create one of his urban residential developments as part of the overall scheme. Laura Trudeau, senior program director for the foundation, said Kresge believes that restoring natural streams in urban areas has multiple benefits. "Having open water in a city neighborhood is a real amenity for folks," she told me.

Vogel is the first to admit that daylighting takes time, skill, and dollars. It requires knowledge of water dynamics, topography, structural engineering, and other fields, and it raises political questions about what neighbors need and want.

"You don't send a backhoe out and just start digging," Vogel said. "You have to build computer models of flows and all that kind of stuff, and all that's yet to be done."

But Baron and other backers remain big fans of the concept. Based on demand, the Bloody Run watershed could become a center for recreation, wind and solar panel farms, and urban agriculture, as well as more traditional economic development.

"It's the kind of transformational effort that really could help and create some real sense of excitement in the city," Baron said. "There's an economic development strategy that could be developed around it, with new green technology, and really take that area and completely reformulate it in a way that's not been done with any major city in the country."

The historic Bloody Run was fed by rainwater and ran from north of Eastern Market south to the Detroit River. Vogel has mapped out a plan to restore the stream by creating rainwater ponds along the route that would release water into the creek when it is running dry. Vogel said putting rainwater into the stream instead of into city sewers could keep more than two billion gallons of water per year out of the sewer system.

Restoring Bloody Run would mean routing it around existing development through mostly vacant areas. Vogel terms it following "the path of least resistance, but still [being] as close as we can to the historical setting."

Vogel, Baron, and other planners have suggested a pilot project be tried first in an area in mostly vacant land east of the city's Eastern Market. Money for it would likely come from private foundations or the federal government, since the financially strapped city government doesn't have the resources.

Despite the preliminary nature of the idea, backers of restoring Detroit's historic streams remain enthusiastic.

"When the French came [to Detroit], they called it paradise because it was such a lush landscape," Nethercott said. "And it's true. We have river and forest and stream and marsh and plain. And we need to start to see Detroit as a fertile place. That'll change everything."

"The question is when can this all come together, and I don't know how to answer that question," Vogel said during our conversation alongside a small remnant of the creek that still runs on the surface in Detroit's Elmwood Cemetery. "My long history would make me somewhat cynical and say it will take years. On the other hand, I see it happening in other cities. I don't know why it couldn't start next year."

Despite the complexities and the lack of an obvious source of money, Vogel takes courage from the enthusiasm of his students, whom he finds more socially conscious now—more like his generation going to school in the '60s.

"I've reached the age where I know that the city is for the young, and a lot of young people are coming in, and I am hopeful that this time a difference can be made," he told me. "I have spent forty years of my career trying to make a difference, and I wish I was thirty years old right now because I feel something is actually going to happen."

ARTS TO THE RESCUE

Artist Mitch Cope and his architect wife Gina Reichert moved into their working-class Detroit neighborhood at precisely the wrong time, at least from a real-estate perspective. The Great Recession was about to hit, riddling their modest but mostly occupied neighborhood with foreclosures and abandoned homes. But if their timing wasn't great from the standpoint of making money, it was perfect for seizing an opportunity to work out a new vision for urban spaces.

They started by buying a single house a block from their own. Two stories, wood framed, dating to the 1920s, the house typified the solid working-class homes that filled up Detroit's vast spaces as the automotive industry boomed. Cope and Reichert bought it out of foreclosure for nineteen hundred dollars, borrowing the money from Cope's dad. They dubbed it the PowerHouse and set about making it the most energy-efficient home in Detroit. That meant major surgery, ripping out walls and adding more trusses to the attic. They scrounged old blackboards from a nearby abandoned school to use as backsplashes in the remade kitchen. An abandoned pool table in the neighborhood became a slate countertop. When it's finished, electricity will come from solar panels and a wind turbine on the roof, heat from a wood-burning stove downstairs and generous south-facing windows upstairs. There'll be a composting toilet. The water supply will come from cisterns and filters.

"The idea of the house is an experiment to see what do you need to be successfully off the grid in Detroit and what will it cost," Cope told me during a visit in early 2012. "We're hoping the whole project will be no more than eighty thousand dollars. We picked that number because that's what the mortgage was foreclosed on."

Having started with one house, Cope and Reichert and their like-minded friends bought others in the immediate neighborhood, inviting artists from as far away as The Netherlands to join them in the project. As of early 2012, PowerHouse Productions, their nonprofit entity, owned seven homes and more than a dozen vacant lots. Each house they remake gets a theme. There's the Sound House, slated to become a music recording studio, and the Squash House, which will become a regulation squash court on the inside, while the vacant lot next door will become an urban garden for growing—what else?— squash. Cope and Reichert were planning a Write House, to be given to the

Artist Mitch Cope and his wife are recruiting artists to revitalize a neighborhood in Detroit scarred by abandonment and foreclosures. (Author photo)

writer of the best essay about why they should get the house. (The winner will also get some help fixing it up, Cope said, "So it's not, 'You win this award and then you get a huge problem.'")

All these houses get what might be called the Heidelberg Treatment, the use of paint and found objects attached to the exteriors of homes in the manner of Detroit's famed Heidelberg Project outdoor art installation. At the first PowerHouse, Cope attached vinyl siding "wings" to an abandoned boat to create a futuristic craft perched in the vacant lot next to the house. "One of the ideas is obviously to beautify the house, but also keep it really secure," Cope said. "The long-term goal is sustainability but also maintenance and security. One of the issues in Detroit obviously is that with all these homes you end up having issues with crime and sustainability and energy and efficiency all at once."

In the vacant lots of the neighborhood, PowerHouse Productions is trying out a range of tactics, creating urban gardens or tree farms or skateboarding parks. More than a dozen lots are in some stage of reclamation from the weeds and the rusted automobiles. One lot they worked on was next to a drug house, and, as Riet Schumack found in Brightmoor, fixing up vacant lots and empty houses tends to drive out the drug users. On the lot across the street from the first PowerHouse, Cope planted a type of plant known as a ghetto palm (Ailanthus altissima) for its hardiness and ability to grow even in small cracks in a sidewalk. "We're trying to civilize these weed trees," he told me with a smile.

By now, after three years of effort, the PowerHouse project has demonstrated how artists and their energy can halt the urban slide and help reverse it. No one would say PowerHouse has created a paradise; real-estate values in that corner of Detroit remain among the poorest in urban America, and foreclosures still scar the district. But the core inspiration prevails—to take an urban space that otherwise would be all or mostly abandoned and turn it into something inspiringly new.

The grandfather of all such artistic efforts in Detroit is of course Heidelberg, created by Tyree Guyton in his rapidly unraveling eastside neighborhood as a protest against blight and abandonment. With his trademark polka dots, found objects, and original art, the Heidelberg Project has taken over a full city block and is spilling out the edges to nearby lots. The art project celebrated its twenty-fifth anniversary in 2011. An effort initially scorned by the city, which bulldozed it twice in the early years, Heidelberg is now recognized as a leading tourist attraction. Guyton's work is part of the collection of the Detroit Institute of Arts, and the artist himself was spending part of 2011–2012 in Basel, Switzerland, on an international artist fellowship.

So wherein do we find the power of art to remake an abandoned urban space? It operates on many levels. Art delivers a dash of energy and color, transforming vacant lots and abandoned homes from dreary backdrop to hard-to-miss objects of interest. Then, too, artists like the cheap living and studio space to be found in vacant urban spaces. And artists tend to be creative thinkers with a social conscience, willing to connect with the remaining urban residents in conversations across lines of race and class. When the broader public visits a place like Heidelberg, not everyone gets the art right away, but everyone feels the shock of urgency in what otherwise would be just an empty, colorless urban space.

"I think the most powerful message is that as a community we had allowed ourselves to become discarded," Jenenne Whitfield, the Heidelberg Project's

Dr. Valentino Castellani, the former mayor of Turin, Italy, stops to snap a photo of Detroit's Heidelberg Project during the American Assembly meetings in Detroit. (Author photo)

executive director, told me during a visit in late 2011. "But what happens when you pick these things up, dust them off, rearrange them, add color? You literally breathe new life into those things, and hence we are breathing new life into our community."

In recent years, the Heidelberg Project has moved well beyond a venue for a single artist's imagination. Guyton invites fellow artists like Chazz Miller, a muralist based in Detroit's Old Redford district, to add his own work to the vast outdoor playscape. Guyton frequently asks visitors (including this author) to add a polka dot to one of the houses in the street as a way to connect everyone in a common endeavor. And Heidelberg Project's staff of volunteers helps coordinate a host of art events and music performances for audiences who might otherwise not get to enjoy something like that.

Jessica Williams, a young Detroit native, helped developed the Young Association of Heidelberg, working with young adults who are interested in using art to change their communities. She told me how when she turned

The more Detroit loses population, the more the remaining residents make their mark with guerrilla art projects and other alterations to the urban landscape, like this "Memory Field" ground sculpture. (Author photo)

eighteen she couldn't wait to leave Detroit for college elsewhere. "I was one of those eighteen-year-olds who said there's was nothing here for me," she said. Studying art at the University of Michigan in Ann Arbor, she discovered Heidelberg, first through a documentary and then by visiting. "I was confronted by my own lack of knowledge about my own city, about the people that actually are here changing it into something that other eighteen-year-olds like myself would no longer hate," she said. "From that initial visit, I said to myself I have to do something that would change my city, so that there would be other young adults who would want to stay here."

Whitfield likes to call it the "spiral effect," something that starts within a community and spirals outward and has a reverberating effect on the whole community. "So it's very symbolic, very magical," she said. "It provokes thought, it provokes questions, and that is part of the magic of this work."

Nowhere is the power of art to salvage an empty urban space better demonstrated than in Philadelphia, where the celebrated Mural Arts Program has created some thirty-six hundred indoor and outdoor murals since its creation in 1984 as an anti-graffiti program. Then-mayor Wilson Goode hired Jane Golden, an artist and muralist from California, to run an art component of the program.

"I was hired at a very exciting time in Philadelphia," Golden told me when I visited her in 2011. "Wilson was our first African American mayor, the city had been filled with blight and graffiti, many of the neighborhoods have been neglected, and Goode came along and made promises that he was going to change things. So there was this incredible spirit in the air." Goode formed the Anti-Graffiti Network and hired Golden to run its small art component. "I don't think anyone understood just how much talent and interest existed amongst the graffiti writers," she said. "For me, as an artist who has been doing murals in Los Angeles, it was incredible to see all this potential that had gone unrecognized." She started working with graffiti artists to create murals throughout the city, and eventually her little program grew and grew. When the city's official anti-graffiti effort closed down in 1997, the Mural Arts Program spun off into a quasi-public nonprofit that gets forty percent of its funding from the city and the rest from donations.

To visit Philadelphia today is to be astonished at the variety and quality of the city's murals. They range from small murals on the sides of one-story structures in the neighborhoods to multistory works on the sides of downtown buildings. Mural Arts creates about one hundred new murals a year. It has more than a thousand kids in an after-school arts program. It conducts art workshops with six hundred inmates at seven prisons. Golden, who still runs Mural Arts today, gets calls from hundreds of cities in the United States who want to emulate her success; in recent years, she has worked with Paris, Hanoi, Dublin, and London on mural projects. In Philadelphia alone, Mural Arts keeps a waiting list of two thousand people and neighborhood groups that want a mural. Strangers approach Golden in the grocery store, telling her they have been on her waiting list for years. The program employs sixty-two full-time staffers, and pays some three hundred artists a year to work on murals.

Golden herself grew up in what she calls a mural-friendly family, with parents who loved the Depression-era artists like Thomas Hart Benton. She thought of practicing law, but the call of the art world was too strong.

When I moved into Los Angeles after I graduated from college and I saw these glorious murals in L.A., I started to think about how murals make art accessible to everyone and how important that notion is. So I decided to put off law school, and I applied for this little grant to do a mural in Santa Monica, and as this mural started to unfold there, I was talking to people about neighborhood politics, community issues, personal concerns, and suddenly I realized that it wasn't theoretical anymore about what murals do. This was the reality that art was able to move people and inspire people.

Cesar Viveros has helped create about three dozen large murals across Philadelphia. Born in Veracruz, Mexico, he told me he didn't have much opportunity to work as an artist there, but once he drifted to Philadelphia, he blossomed within the Mural Arts Program. On the day I met him in late 2011, he was finishing a butterfly-themed mural on the side of a recreation center building, but his biggest contribution perhaps is his Healing Walls mural. It grew out of Jane Golden's wish to engage the community fully, and since crime remained a scourge in the city, she engaged Viveros to work with both victims and prison inmates to envision a mural.

The process became a scalding emotional process for all, as men doing life in prison without parole for murder met the families of their victims.

"In a way I was quite naïve," Golden told me. "I didn't realize the amount of acrimony that would be stirred up, and at some point I said to myself, I am a layperson, what in the world did I get into. I seem to just have done nothing but open up wounds." But the meetings continued inside the prisons. Golden created teams, each consisting of four crime victims or their family members and four inmates, each working at a table in a prison auditorium. "And that's when things started to percolate," she said. "It was when people started to create together and communicate. There is something about art that is incredibly meaningful and inspiring and engaging, that makes people see beyond the typical boundaries and borders that divide all of us."

The result was Healing Walls, a mural by Viveros on the theme of remorse and forgiveness. On the left, prison inmates occupy a quiet, contemplative space, dropping seeds through their cell bars, while to the right we see victims and families, children who are growing up without fathers, women who don't

Mexican-born muralist Cesar Viveros works on a mural in Philadelphia on behalf of Jane Golden's Mural Arts program. (Author photo)

The Healing Wall mural in Philadelphia by Cesar Viveros depicts inmates and victims' families. Note that Philadelphia Green with one of its trademark rail fences has reclaimed the vacant lot. (Author photo)

have husbands, shadows of their former selves. And there is a tree growing that represents the strength and resilience of the community.

Often the Mural Arts program creates an artwork on a wall facing one of the vacant lots reclaimed by Bob Grossmann's Philadelphia Green program. So on a single lot in Philadelphia we can witness both vacant lot restoration and public art joining together to remake an abandoned urban space into a real public amenity.

Who Decides?

Underlying the question of what to do with vacant urban land is an even more baseline issue: *Who* gets to decide, and *how* are decisions made? People who ignore such questions do so at their peril. Half a century ago, urban planning was largely something done to poorer city residents by those in power; and, of course, nobody today (well, almost nobody) looks back at urban renewal in the 1950s and '60s as a successful endeavor. Neighborhood redevelopment works when it engages the people on the ground, in the neighborhood, on the issues that concern them. The act of listening becomes more than a nod to social justice and equity; it becomes the most practical way of coming up with a workable solution.

In Youngstown, Ohio, in the early years of the 2000s, then-mayor Jay Williams led the political fight to create Youngstown 2010, the justly famous plan to reshape the city as a smaller, greener city. Youngstown, one of the steel-making capitals of the world, saw its economy collapse after the mills closed in the late 1970s; the population slid from a high near 190,000 in 1970 to under 70,000 today. Williams, a native of the city and a banker by trade, ran for mayor preaching a gospel of reinvention as a smaller but better city; but he recognized that creating an actual plan would demand full involvement by city residents. Every issue got a full hearing. Williams and other civic leaders engaged in lengthy debates and discussions on race relations and social justice. The process took three full years. Hunter Morrison, a professor of planning at Youngstown State University who helped lead the discussions and develop the plan, told me during an interview that he knew he had reached a state of "planner's Nirvana" when somebody at a meeting asked if they hadn't discussed all the issues enough and wasn't it time to move on with the plan.

Since the creation of Youngstown 2010, the city has found its plan difficult to implement, largely because of inadequate resources within city government and within the city itself. But the city has learned to target its resources carefully, and Youngstown 2010 remains notable around the world as one of the earliest efforts to acknowledge shrinkage and embrace a city's fate as a smaller—but hopefully better—place.

Contrast the painstaking approach to envisioning new uses for vacant land in Youngstown with the Detroit Works project launched by Mayor Dave Bing in late summer 2010. Hailed as a brave attempt by a visionary mayor to make the tough decisions needed in Detroit, the effort soon faltered. Public meetings, at which city officials admittedly were not prepared for what happened, deteriorated into mass gripe sessions at which hundreds of citizens unwilling to talk about long-range plans complained about poor city services instead. At a second round of hearings, city leaders gave residents hand-held devices to "click" answers to questions posed during a slide show; but the questions were so basic and the lack of true engagement with the audience so palpable that few left satisfied. "I felt I was being led," complained Maggie DeSantis, president of the nonprofit Warren-Conner Development Coalition and a longtime neighborhood leader on Detroit's east side.

As it happened, DeSantis and her colleagues were then engaged in a project of their own that could serve as a model of true community engagement on vacant land. Known as LEAP, for the Lower Eastside Action Plan, the effort sent teams of volunteers into neighborhoods to survey thousands of residents, invited citizens to meetings at which they could pore over maps and suggest appropriate new uses for vacant parcels, and generally stayed with the process for well over a year before presenting its detailed findings and suggestions. Although for political reasons nobody wanted to draw sharp comparisons with Detroit Works, it was clear to many that LEAP proved the better model. As Ayana Rhodes-Ako, a Detroit resident and LEAP volunteer, told me, "You're actually talking to the neighbors and you're talking to the people that live in the community, in comparison to the Detroit Works project where they're having consultants coming in and making assessments based on whatever data that they're using, the census or whatever, when they need to knock on doors and really talk to people." The LEAP effort was so well done, and so inclusive of the

citizens, that Bing's Detroit Works long-term planning program later evolved
to emulate a more LEAP-like community-engagement approach. The new
approach was more inclusive, but it remains to be seen, as I write this in 2012,
how much of the community engagement work will find its way into city policy
in the years ahead.

The LEAP project grew out of a desire of three nonprofit community
groups—Warren-Conner Development Coalition, Jefferson East Business
Association, and Genesis HOPE Community Development—to find new uses
for rapidly expanding vacant land on the east side. With about three hundred
thousand dollars in funding from the Erb Foundation and other backers, the
LEAP team worked with several outside experts—landscape architects from
Ann Arbor-based JJR, demographers from Data Driven Detroit, legal help from
Community Legal Resources, and more—to help guide the discussions.

Among the ideas being considered for the area's most vacant expanses are
storm water retention ponds, reforestation, urban farms, wineries, and green
zones, as well as using decommissioned schools as food processing plants.
Those are merely concepts now, but DeSantis said the LEAP project hopes for
solid plans to emerge, not just fanciful ideas. "We don't want pretty pictures,"
she said. "We want a set of strategies that work."

Khalil Ligon, LEAP's staff director, acknowledged that many residents hold
out hope for complete rehabilitation of their neighborhoods, a return to Detroit's
glory years. But Ligon and other leaders were willing to think anew.

"Of course, everybody wants a traditional residential neighborhood, but the
reality is, that's not going to happen," she told me in 2011. "Our population [in
the LEAP study area] went from sixty-plus thousand to thirty-plus thousand in
ten years. So we've been on a continuing decline. I think we have to be realistic
about the type of neighborhoods we can have."

LEAP, like an earlier study of neighborhood types developed by the nonprofit
Community Development Advocates of Detroit—and like the later Detroit Works
long-term planning team—maintained that every Detroit district, no matter how
vacant and abandoned, has a proper and useful role to play.

"Even if you can't have a house on every block, that doesn't mean that this is
not a viable neighborhood, that it can't be something positive to come out of it,"

Many Detroit residents today remain deeply involved in the fate of their city. Here citizens help define the route of new greenways on the lower east city. (Author photo)

Ligon told me. "We just have to redefine how we use that space and find people who want to stay in that particular land-use type."

A Generative Landscape

The key to all these new uses—art and farming and daylighted streams—is that vacant urban land offers us an opportunity, not just a problem. Vacancy allows us to create better cities not in spite of being smaller but because they're smaller; vacancy opens up possibilities otherwise closed off to us.

We've developed a few rough guidelines for new urban land uses. We should be thinking in terms of what urban planner Constance Bodurow of Lawrence Technological University calls a generative landscape—a landscape that, in the absence of traditional market demand, produces food and jobs through urban farms, or electricity through great fields of solar panels. Whatever use we decide on must be self-sustaining, since our municipal governments are too weak and too broke to underwrite these projects. We need to remake our legal system when it comes to urban land—that whole apparatus of planning and zoning and clearing titles and the like—since things like side lots and art projects and urban farms are taking place without the benefit in most places of legal formalities, and we ought to encourage these uses rather than stymie them. And the remaining residents in our cities must have a real say in what happens, for urban neighborhoods in places like Youngstown and Flint aren't whiteboards in a planning seminar, but places where real people have stuck it out.

Cities have always occupied the best ground. That ground is still there, vacant now perhaps, but awaiting new uses and new passions.

LEARNING FROM EUROPE

LESSONS FROM BRITAIN AND GERMANY

In late 2010, just before I flew to Europe to study shrinking cities there, I was telling my editor at the *Detroit Free Press* about my hopes for the trip. European cities had gained a lead on US cities; they were rebuilding post-industrial cities like Leipzig, Germany, and Manchester, England, far more quickly than we Americans had done facing similar ills in Detroit and Flint and Youngstown. My editor gave me a skeptical look. "It's easy for them to make progress," he said. "They're socialist." He meant, of course, that Euro-zone communities accustomed to high taxes and regulatory oversight would more readily accept massive government intervention—that a few central planners could impose their will far more easily than in America.

By the time I returned to the newsroom following my trip, I could report that the cities I had visited had progressed not through central government planning, but by embracing a spirit of innovation and entrepreneurship. And indeed the most interesting projects that I saw, and the ones with the most to offer American cities hungry for ideas, were the ones where government had played a minor role at best, usually by facilitating work and then getting out of the way.

It's an open question whether US and European cities can actually learn from each other; perhaps our very real cultural differences mean that progress made in, say, Turin, Italy, or Germany's Ruhr Valley, both devastated industrial areas remaking themselves in new and creative ways, would be difficult if not impossible to emulate in America. But the European model is worth our attention, if only to see real-life examples of cities overcoming some of the very same challenges that the Detroits of the world face.

MANCHESTER, ENGLAND

If any city can claim to be the home and epicenter of the Industrial Revolution, that city is Manchester. Today the third-largest city in England, Manchester was a provincial center in the early 1800s when entrepreneurs began building cotton mills in and around the city, connected by a network of canals and the world's first railway, the Manchester-Liverpool line, built in 1830. Wealth and work drew in more people; the city's population doubled and doubled again by the mid-nineteenth century. Already the cotton capital of the world, Manchester added more industry through the decades—chemicals and mining and steel, the workers crammed into tenements in the shadows of the giant factories, their plight the inspiration for Friedrich Engels's "The Condition of the Working Class in England" as early as the 1840s.

Industrial decline set in as early as World War I, as fighting restricted cotton shipments. Aging factories, rising costs, and foreign competition—all familiar to Detroiters a few decades later—bit into Manchester's leadership role. By the 1960s, the losses of jobs and industry became a free fall. Aerial photographs of a district known as East Manchester, not far from the central downtown, show dense concentrations of factories in the 1940s but a moonscape of empty fields a few decades later. The city's population dwindled from around 750,000 in 1930 to barely 400,000 in the 1990s.

Adding insult to injury, the Irish Republican Army set off a bomb in downtown Manchester in June 1996. One of the IRA's biggest bombings ever, it destroyed whole blocks of the downtown, although no one died thanks to the IRA's practice of giving prior warning to evacuate people. The bomb could have finished the city off, much as Katrina all but destroyed New Orleans. Instead those demolished blocks of the downtown provided opportunities for renewal, the explosion a catalyst for the city to think anew and act anew.

The change in attitude had already begun. As times worsened and unemployment soared in the 1970s and '80s, Mancunians (as residents are known) had demanded that the central government in London shower them with government aid. But the weakness of Britain's Labour Party during the Thatcherite years led to a revision of thinking, and the IRA bombing merely accelerated that change. Sir Richard Leese, the long-term leader of the Manchester governing council (the equivalent of mayor), explained to my group of visiting Americans in late 2010 that by the early '90s city leaders turned away from civic socialism toward a more pro-business entrepreneurial approach. What he called Manchester's "Cambodian period" was over. "The only way we were going to create jobs was through the private sector," Leese said.

As in so many other cities, much of the new development was led by the young and the hip. Musicians and recording companies took advantage of the cheap warehouses and loft spaces in the central downtown; soon the city enjoyed a flourishing local music scene, known as "Madchester" for its recording studios and record labels. A bar and club scene developed; the student population soared at Manchester's universities; a liberal atmosphere welcomed gay bars and clubs. Loft living became a trend.

In the devastated East Manchester district, the city envisioned a new sports complex arising. It bid on the 1996 Olympics but lost; but Manchester did win the right to host the 2002 Commonwealth Games, an event nearly as large and as prestigious. The city built a range of new arenas on the former industrial land. Today the Manchester City soccer team calls home the largest of the new facilities (the team is not to be confused with its more famous crosstown rivals, Manchester United). Other development followed the games; new housing and high-tech digital industry filled out the district.

Government leaders did not try to steer new business development in any particular direction, but rather let entrepreneurs choose their way.

"You can't stop the market from doing things it wants to do," Ian Slater, deputy chief executive of New East Manchester, a quasi-public agency working to develop the district, told us during our visit.

One small project provided for me a startling contrast with Detroit's way of doing things. In the East Manchester district, planners converted an empty industrial building into incubator space for new digital entrepreneurs, with a board overseeing the project consisting mostly of private-sector individuals. In the vast open warehouse portion of the building, they had thought of building out cubicles for small start-up firms; but instead simply lined up rows of empty shipping containers converted with glass fronts and electricity. These they rented out to digital entrepreneurs for as little as about one hundred dollars a month. Empty shipping containers stack up in cities the world over; once their cargoes of grain and other goods are removed, the containers are too expensive

Weekenders throng downtown Manchester for the shopping, pubs, and other entertainment. (Author photo)

to send back empty to China or wherever. Europeans have gotten creative at reusing these empty containers for schools, housing, and other structures; the structures they create often look like purpose-built buildings instead of a stack of empty boxes. In the East Manchester warehouse, each entrepreneurial firm may get no more than a couple of hundred square feet, but for a one-to-three-person operation, that's all they need. Katie Gallagher (no relation to this author), the business manager of the incubator operation when I visited, told us she had expected to lease out two or three of the container spaces the first month; instead entrepreneurs snapped up dozens of them, and they showed no signs of leaving. "I think we're going to have to get them out with shoehorns," she said. And of course the possibilities for networking inherent in all those start-up firms sharing the same environment created yet more benefits.

Using shipping containers in this innovative way contrasts sharply with a similar project in Detroit, in which private developers have proposed using empty shipping containers to create a rental housing project. The idea was

Unrecognizable now for what they once were, these empty shipping containers have been converted to office space at a business incubator in Manchester, England. (Author photo)

proposed in 2008 but has languished since then. The nation's real-estate bust and credit crunch gets a lot of the blame, but so also does the city's calcified planning process, which didn't know what to do with a project so different from the norm.

David Rudlin, an urban planner in Manchester, told me that the city readily allows business development that other cities might try to regulate more heavily, such as allowing tall buildings to rise in and around the historic architecture of the city center. In Manchester, he said, "The tall building policy is, 'Yes, please.'" Civic leaders also try to show a welcoming face to the large immigrant population (again, in contrast to many American cities). Leese explained that the city has adopted a slogan to welcome all who can contribute: "It's not where you're from, it's where you're at."

When the British central government in London decreed that the BBC network had to move at least part of its operations out of the capital to other cities as a way of spreading the wealth, Manchester was ready with its bid.

Former shipping containers converted to entrepreneurial pods at a Manchester, England, business incubator. (Author photo)

The BBC now operates in a strikingly modern office complex in the downtown area, and to encourage digital communications spinoffs, the city has been trying to achieve a policy of being fully wired with the latest high-speed broadband connections.

Certainly Manchester's fall from grace spurred all this new creative thinking. "A place needs a crisis narrative," Mike Emmerich, chief executive of Manchester's quasi-public Commission for the New Economy, told us. "We've been sweating a model of civic entrepreneurship bloody hard for twenty years now." And Manchester tries to anticipate future developments and be ready to meet them. As Emmerich put it, "When the [London] government comes up with another stupid idea, Manchester always has projects on the shelf ready to go. That's leadership."

Leese and the other civic leaders all readily admit that Manchester remains a troubled city, a work in progress. Poverty remains high, trapping generations of

Downtown Manchester has become home to Britain's BBC network regional offices as well as spinoff developments in housing, retail, and commercial real estate. (Author photo)

families and limiting the social mobility of lower-class individuals. Gentrification has pushed poorer families out of some districts without giving them anyplace to go; as a writer named Phil Misselwitz puts it, "The problem of social deprivation appears to be pushed out of the city rather than solved." The most distressed parts of Manchester still see long-term unemployment running well into double digits. And Mancunians appear to have not given up on the dream of government largesse; during the week I visited the city, demonstrators clashed with police over the national government's cuts in education spending.

What Manchester has accomplished isn't a Nirvana, but a sustained, realistic effort to generate new ways of thinking and acting at the civic leadership level. The ability to coalesce around a unified vision, to direct resources toward that vision, to partner with the private sector rather than trying to control it—all these have made Manchester what many like to call the "fastest-growing shrinking city" in Britain.

LEIPZIG, GERMANY

What Katrina did to New Orleans, the fall of communism did to Leipzig.

The second-largest city in East Germany during the Cold War, Leipzig had long enjoyed a reputation as a center of learning, celebrated as the home of J.S. Bach and with a university that dated to 1409. Less a manufacturing center than a locus of commerce and trade, Leipzig hosted one of Europe's most famous trade fairs; its outdoor Christmas markets filled the streets of the central downtown each December. The population peaked at about 713,000 in 1933, then steadily declined through the war years and during the socialist German Democratic Republic era, as political power flowed to East Berlin and Leipzig's status as a regional capital diminished. Even so, Leipzig's central downtown had survived World War II more or less intact, and so retained its Old World architecture and charm. The city's population stood at 530,000 in 1989 when the Berlin Wall opened.

The Christmastime shopping scene in downtown Leipzig, Germany, is alive with lights, people, up-scale retail, and outdoor displays. Many of the stores are new since German reunification. (Author photo)

German reunification the following year changed everything. Leipzig's economic base, in textiles, publishing, and metalworking, had been propped up by the old Soviet Bloc economic system; now those industries all but collapsed overnight. Leipzig boasted about one hundred thousand manufacturing jobs in 1989; two years later, that roster had dwindled to just ten thousand. Whole industries vanished. The *Treuhandanstalt*, the agency set up to privatize the state-owned industrial conglomerates, bungled the job in many cases; in Leipzig, of eight hundred such companies privatized, almost three hundred closed. A huge heavy-machinery manufacturer called Takraf, when privatized, saw its workforce shrink from 5,000 to 250.

Then, too, Leipzig residents, long restricted from moving to West Germany or even to suburban areas by law and tight housing constraints, started to leave. Leipzig lost one hundred thousand residents, or about twenty percent of its population, in a short time. Half of those residents moved into newly built housing estates in nearby suburbs; large numbers of people went to the more prosperous West Germany, and of course many of those were the younger, more economically skilled workers. The leave-taking resulted in a huge overhang of vacant and often obsolete housing in the central city; by the year 2000, about twenty percent of Leipzig's housing stock stood empty. Social problems mounted; the city's unemployment rate jumped from about eight percent in 1990 to nearly twenty-five percent fifteen years later, twice that of the German nation at large. Hinrich Lehmann-Grube, who became Leipzig's mayor in 1990 and helped spark reform, told me during my visit in late 2010 that in 1990 the city was "stinking, dirty, polluted. It was rather terrible."

Leipzig had found itself, in short, identified as a prototype of a shrinking city; its plight helped spark the interest of scholars and urban planners in such places, first in Germany, then in the wider Europe, then in the American Rust Belt, and finally worldwide.

Perhaps because it suffered more than most, Leipzig soon adopted one of Europe's most progressive programs toward renewal. It involved wide leveraging of relief dollars from the German government; aggressive legal stratagems to combat vacancy; widespread greening of surplus urban land; strict targeting of limited resources; and an entrepreneurial approach toward attracting new business.

Leipzig, Germany, like American Rust Belt cities, is trying to replace its lost industry by nurturing start-up companies in incubators like this one. (Author photo)

Start with the legal stratagems. Having lost ten percent of its population to newly built suburbs, Leipzig annexed those suburbs, regaining the lost population. At the same time, under reunification, German laws held that properties taken by the old East German government had to be returned to their original owners, who could not just be compensated with tax dollars; that stymied much inner-city redevelopment work because the properties were tied up in title disputes. So leaders changed the law. The city of Leipzig gained control of thousands of buildings; those beyond saving were demolished, while many thousands of rental apartments were modernized.

Green belts were established close to the city center, and more are planned. Leipzig filled in disused mining pits in the south of the city with water, creating lakefront property. The city's downtown train station, one of Europe's largest, kept its trains but was remade as a destination shopping mall, too. A large new modern art museum was built nearby. Downtown living became trendy;

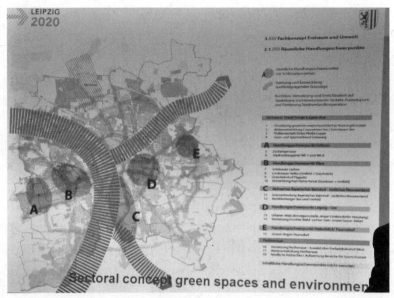

Leipzig urban planners are taking advantage of industrial loss and population flight by mapping out green belts in the city. (Author photo)

the population began to grow again after 2000, nudging above five hundred thousand again.

Leipzig leaders also determined to attract new industry with a pro-business attitude, offering access to open land, cross-departmental cooperation, and increased services to potential investors and businesses. BMW chose Leipzig for its new manufacturing site over 250 cities that had sought it.

One small but representative program seemed to capture the spirit of the effort. By 2010, Leipzig had created a few dozen "guardian houses," vacant and dilapidated buildings that the city gave rent-free to nonprofit groups; the idea was that artists and other urban pioneers could live and work in the buildings rent-free in exchange for fixing up the properties. Most of these structures would not meet codes by US standards, and it was hard to imagine a US city blessing such a project, but Leipzig moved ahead anyway.

One of the most dramatic changes occurred at Spinnerei, Leipzig's huge textile complex, measuring some 750,000 square feet of industrial space. When communism fell and the market for its textiles collapsed, Spinnerei began to empty out; within a couple of years, the workers were gone. But artists soon began to move in, attracted by the low cost and ample open spaces. Today the Spinnerei artist colony nearly fills out the old industrial space with a host of studios, galleries, and related tenants. Earlier I quoted Wennemar de Weldige, a project coordinator with the City of Leipzig's Department of Economic Development, on this project, but it's worth repeating: During my visit to Spinnerei, he said the city permitted the burgeoning artists colony to remake the complex with little or no oversight from city regulators. With little money to offer the artists as incentives, de Weldige said, "We can give only freedom."

As in Manchester, the progress has not transformed Leipzig into anybody's idea of a paradise. Unemployment and poverty rates remain high; large parts of the city still suffer from vacancy. Europe's new fiscal austerity at all levels of government limits the ability of even the smartest civic leaders to carry out new projects. But like Manchester, Leipzig today offers a prime example of a city knocked to the floor by history's toughest punch, only to resurrect itself through smart thinking, committed leadership, and a sheer refusal to die.

THE DIFFERENCE WITH US CITIES

To get back to my editor's skepticism about Europe, I admit I did see many cultural differences between Leipzig/Manchester and US cities. But my editor's crack about socialism had nothing to do with it. Some of the key differences include:

Europeans Believe in Cities, while Americans Believe in Suburbs

From the beginnings of suburban sprawl in the years after World War II, American leadership at all levels promoted suburban growth. Federal money built new roads and expressways in suburbia; federal mortgage subsidies promoted suburban construction; banks and insurance companies redlined urban neighborhoods while flooding newer suburban communities with cash. The home-building and retail industries abandoned older urban districts in favor of suburban tract housing and shopping malls. The fragmented government in places like metropolitan Detroit, where more than two hundred villages, townships, cities, school districts, and counties all enjoy home-rule autonomy, makes regional cooperation difficult at best.

Contrast that with what I saw in Leipzig. Shortly after the fall of communism, tens of thousands of Leipzig residents moved out of town—some to the newly opened western Germany, but others to newly built housing developments in the suburbs. Government responded by promptly allowing Leipzig to annex those suburbs, regaining some fifty thousand or so residents they had lost. Laws that inhibited redevelopment of vacant residential buildings in the city's core were amended to make redevelopment easier. Resources poured in. "Over forty years, we have defined urban redevelopment as bipartisan," said Oliver Weigel, an official with the Federal Ministry of Transport, Building, and Urban Development. "Consensus is our strength." And then, more tellingly, he added, "We definitely try to make people look foolish if they move out of town. . . . It's uncool to move out of town."

American urban experts like Christopher Leinberger of the Brookings Institution have proclaimed that a new interest in walkable urbanism leaves American cities poised for a comeback. But I find that walkable urban neighborhoods remain a niche market for now, enclaves that attract a variety of young people and empty nesters—the "never wed and almost dead," as some say. Most of the home-buying public seems content to reside out in suburbia. And certainly the vast imbalance in federal support for highways over mass transit shows that government policy continues to undergird suburban sprawl.

Europe Is Less Litigious than America

In Leipzig, examples like the guardian houses struck the Americans in my group as hard to replicate in the US. What about code violations in these structures? What about liability issues? Accustomed to American municipal bureaucracy, we could think of a host of constraints that would delay, if not block, such a free-wheeling experiment. One of my group, Bob Brown, the director of planning for the City of Cleveland, told Leipzig officials, "We'd all like to copy this. We're trying to figure out how to make it happen."

The answer from the bemused German officials was that they didn't have to worry about lawsuits as American officials did; that European society was much less litigious. Everyone accepted that a voluntary program like the guardian houses offered opportunities that were worth the risks; that absent such a program, the vacant structures would remain a drag on society. So why not try something?

The contrast with the hyper-cautious climate within Detroit's municipal government and planning bureaucracies struck me forcibly.

European Cities Often Enjoy Stable Leadership and Long-term Vision

In Manchester, Sir Richard Leese has held his office since 1996, a total of sixteen years as I write this, taking over from a colleague who had held it for a similarly long stretch. In Turin, Italy, Valentino Castellani, the reform mayor who helped lead a turnaround after Turin's auto industry collapsed, served two terms and was succeeded by a colleague who shared his vision. Stable leadership allows these cities to develop a long-range vision, such as Manchester's ambition to be the "capital of northern England," or Turin's evolution from gray industrial backwater to one of Europe's cooler cultural capitals.

Contrast that long-term vision and stable leadership with the short-term, election-to-election governing style of US cities, and indeed of American government in general. In the 2008–2010 period, Detroit saw three mayors, from the disgraced Kwame Kilpatrick to his interim replacement Ken Cockrel Jr. to the newly elected Dave Bing. European cities also take a more integrated approach to revitalization, linking housing, business, education, transit, and recreational planning in unified efforts instead of separate silos, as often happens in America.

As Dan Kildee, the land-bank visionary and former Genesee County treasurer in Flint, told me once, "Unfortunately, people in my business think about one year, because that's the budget, or two or four years, because that's their term of office. If we don't think about the next twenty or twenty-five years, we're going to make mistakes."

Alan Mallach, an urban planner based in New Jersey who has studied Detroit and who visited Leipzig and Manchester with me, said European cities have a clear advantage over their US counterparts.

"You're talking about a way of thinking about how local government operates and makes decisions that is just really, really different from how it's done in the US," he said. "The idea that you make decisions for the long haul, that you really make the private sector a full partner in the process, that you have the kind of flexibility that means you can shift gears and do stuff, that's just a totally different way of thinking."

Despite the cultural differences, I believe places like Manchester and Leipzig do have much to teach their American cousins. They show that urban progress is possible, and on a faster schedule than most Americans may think possible. Detroit in fact may be in the early stages of what we will one day recognize as a turnaround equivalent to what's happened in Manchester and Leipzig. But we still have a lot to learn. And if we're not learning from the good judgment and accomplishments of other cities, it's because we're not trying.

CONCLUSION

The Way Forward

Sweet are the uses of adversity.

Shakespeare wrote that line four hundred years ago. The oldest wisdom remains the best. Forced as are we are to reinvent cities, we find new opportunities if we open our eyes. Our creaky city-county-state governance model might give way (or, more likely, be modified) to allow more neighborhood and regional models to emerge, as they already are in Cleveland and Detroit and elsewhere. Schools turning in pathetic performances can grow into academic powerhouses. A century of relying on giant corporations for everything can give way to a more entrepreneurial way of doing business. Our vast stock of vacant urban land can help us make our cities greener and more environmentally sustainable. All this is possible if we accept the challenge of adversity and work in new ways.

The urban heroes we've met in these pages—Riet Schumack, Thomas Maridada, Sue Mosey, Dan Kildee, and many others—did not follow the same path as those who came before them. All showed a willingness to think anew and act anew. Their courage made the difference.

"I think cities can be revitalized," Bob Grossmann of Philadelphia Green told me once. "I think it's a matter of using the things that are opportunities that may not seem to be opportunities, such as blighted land. It's only limited by our imagination and by the will of the people."

And a more somber, if equally valid, way of saying it comes from Hunter Morrison, the veteran urban planner who helped lead Youngstown, Ohio's quest for a new vision for that city.

"It may take you twenty-five years. Hopefully it doesn't," Morrison told me. "But twenty-five years from now will be twenty-five years from now whether you deal with these issues or not."

If I'm an optimist about Detroit, I present one unassailable reason for hopefulness. Over its three hundred-plus years as a city, Detroit has taken good ideas wherever it found them and made them its own. If the city has nurtured many native sons and daughters—Henry Ford, as an example—the city has equally embraced newcomers and their ideas—architects Albert Kahn, Eliel and Eero Saarinen, Minoru Yamasaki; fighters for justice Rosa Parks, Walter Reuther, Grace Lee Boggs; and thousands more, the anonymous tide swelling up from the Deep South and Appalachia to work in auto factories, the immigrants from many lands speaking many tongues who became the city's laborers, business leaders, doctors, entertainers. The city's greatest paintings, Diego Rivera's murals of Ford's Rouge factory, came from the hand of a newcomer to the city; its sports legends—Gordie Howe, Barry Sanders, Justin Verlander—all came to this city from far away. So the notion that Detroiters fear change, fear new ideas, fear the challenge of reinvention, is absurd on its face.

The challenge now is to take a city at the lowest point in its history and make something new, something useful, rise from the ashes. Detroit has done it before, pivoting at each new century to redefine itself, and thereby leading the nation and the world down new paths. The nation and world once again look to Detroit, seeking new directions for cities, awaiting our answer.

Abandonment and recovery: Early morning bikers by the thousands on the city's annual *Tour de Troit* bike ride pass in front of the city's most famous eyesore, the Michigan Central Train Station. (Author photo)

Introduction: Cities Today

Page 3: "This is an international phenomenon." Author interview with Robin Boyle, Detroit, Sept. 26, 2011.

Page 4: Metro Detroit's population. All population figures for US cities in this book are taken from US Census reports available at www.census.gov.

Page 4: The American Assembly. The assembly's final report, "Reinventing America's Legacy Cities: Strategies for Cities Losing Population," can be found at http://americanassembly.org/publication/reinventing-americas-legacy-cities-strategies-cities-losing-population.

Page 6: Homes were getting bigger. Data on the size of new homes provided by the National Association of Homebuilders.

Page 6: Peter Karmanos Jr. anecdote: John Gallagher, "Karmanos' Detroit Odyssey Leads to Era of Hope," *Detroit Free Press*, Dec. 3, 1999.

Page 7: Sunbelt cities growth data: US Census Bureau reports.

Page 8: Number of manufacturers in Detroit: Citizens Research Council of Michigan, "The Fiscal Condition of the City of Detroit," April 2010, page 6. Accessed at www.crcmich.org/PUBLICAT/2010s/2010/rpt361.pdf.

Page 8: Tax base data: Percentages of tax base remaining in central cities are author calculations based on property valuation data provided by regional planning organizations, including the Southeast Michigan Council of Governments (Detroit), the Delaware Valley Regional Planning Commission (Philadelphia-Camden), the Northern Ohio Data and Information Service (Cleveland), and the East-West Gateway Council of Governments (St. Louis).

Page 9: In Detroit, only about forty percent of parcels provide tax revenue. Statistic provided by City of Detroit Assessment Division to the author.

Page 9. Boston trying to tax nonprofits: Michael Rezendes, "Boston Sending 'Tax'

Bills to Major Non-profits," Boston.com, April 24, 2011, accessed at www. boston.com/business/articles/2011/04/24/boston_sends_tax_bills_to_major_ nonprofits/.

Page 10: Sheila Cockrel quote: Author interview, Aug. 15, 2011, Detroit.

Page 10: Alan Mallach paper: Alan Mallach and Eric Scorsone, "Long-Term Stress and Systemic Failure: Taking Seriously the Fiscal Crisis of America's Older Cities," Center for Community Progress, 2011.

Page 11: Bettie Buss. Author interview, Aug. 24, 2011, Livonia, MI.

Page 11: Saginaw figures: Mallach and Scorsone, ibid.

Page 11: Mallach and Scorsone quote: Mallach and Scorsone, ibid.

Page 11: Birmingham, Michigan, per capita tax base: Author calculation based on tax data found at Southeast Michigan Council of Governments Web site, accessed at www.semcog.org/Data_and_Maps.aspx.

Page 12: Harland Bartholomew pamphlet. Harland Bartholomew, "The Present and Ultimate Effect of Decentralization Upon American Cities," The Urban Land Institute, 1940.

Page 13: Manchester quote: Presentation by Mike Emmerich, Commission for New Economy, to German Marshall Fund Cities in Transition delegates, Dec. 10, 2010. Manchester, England.

Chapter 1: Detroit Today

Page 15: Population and homebuilding statistics: Taken from data at Southeast Michigan Council of Governments Web site: www.semcog.org/Data_and_ Maps.aspx.

Page 16: *City on the Move* available on YouTube: www.youtube.com/ watch?v=vUbsw28PCpA.

Page 18: Unemployment rates for Detroit: Taken from Michigan Bureau of Labor Market Information, available at www.milmi.org/.

Page 18: Vacant parcels in the city: Detroit Residential Parcel Survey by Data Driven Detroit, accessed at http://datadrivendetroit.org/projects/ detroit-residential-parcel-survey/. See also John Gallagher, "Many Are Gone, but More Remain," *Detroit Free Press*, Feb. 20, 2010, accessed at datadrivendetroit.org/wp-content/uploads/2010/04/DRPS_Free_Press_022010. pdf.

Page 21: Matthew Piper: Author interview, Jan. 24, 2012, Detroit.

Page 23: Mosey quote: Sherri Welch, "Sue Mosey: Slow and Steady Approach Revitalizes Midtown," *Crain's Detroit Business*, Jan. 16, 2012.

Page 24: Mosey quote: Author interview, Sept. 22, 2011, Detroit.

Page 24: Brightmoor story—Margaret Dewar and Robert Linn, "Remaking Brightmoor," draft of book chapter made available to author by Prof. Dewar.

Page 26. Ken Wolfe: Author interview, Jan. 10, 2012, Detroit.

Page 27: John George: Site visits and author interviews, Nov. 17, 2011, and Feb. 2, 2012, Detroit.

Page 28: Sheila Cockrel: Author interview, Aug. 15, 2011, Detroit.

Page 28: Oakwood Heights anecdote: Site visit and author interviews with residents of Oakwood Heights district, Nov. 2, 2011.

Page 28: Sheila Cockrel quote: Author interview, Aug. 15, 2011, Detroit.

Chapter 2: New Ways to Govern Our Cities

Page 33: University Circle: This section is based on author visits and interview with Chris Ronayne, Oct. 18, 2011, in Cleveland; history of the district found at www.universitycircle.org; see also Michelle Jarboe McFee, "University Circle Stretches Its Boundaries; Leaders Focus on Building up District, Blurring Borders," *The Plain Dealer*, Nov. 16, 2011, accessed at www. cleveland.com/business/index.ssf/2011/11/university_circle_stretches_ it.html.

Page 39: Eastern Market: This section is based on interviews with Jim Sutherland, Aug. 17, 2011, Detroit; Father Norman Thomas, Aug. 24, 2011, Detroit; Dave O'Neil, Aug. 9, 2011, by phone; Sheila Cockrel, Aug. 15, 2011, Detroit; Kate Beebe, July 27, 2011, Detroit; Ed Deeb, April 29, 2011, Detroit; see also John Gallagher, "How Eastern Market Reinvented Itself," *Detroit Free Press*, June 26, 2010; John Gallagher, "Renovated Eastern Market Is a Chic Event Destination," *Detroit Free Press*, Dec. 19, 2009; John Gallagher, "Nonprofit Could Enliven Landmark," *Detroit Free Press*, May 7, 2006.

Page 53: The Land Bank: This section is based on several conversations with Dan Kildee from 2009 through 2011; Kildee's keynote address to the Land Bank Conference, June 6, 2011, Detroit; author interview with Aundra Wallace, Aug. 25, 2011, Detroit. See also John Gallagher, "The Best Idea

Detroit's Never Tried," chap. 8 in *Reimagining Detroit: Opportunities for Redefining an American City* (Detroit: Wayne State University Press, 2010).

Page 73: Targeting sources: Based on author interviews with Alan Levy, Dec. 12, 2012, by phone; Dale Thompson, Dec. 6, 2011, Dearborn; Peter Zeiler, December 2012, by phone; George Galster, December 2012, Detroit. See also George Galster, Peter Tatian, and John Accordino, "Targeting Investments for Neighborhood Revitalization," *Journal of the American Planning Association* 72, no. 4 (2006): 457–474; Dale Thompson, "Strategic Geographic Targeting in Community Development: Examining the Congruence of Political, Institutional, and Technical Factors," *Urban Affairs Review*, published online March 11, 2011, accessed at http://uar.sagepub.com/content/47/4/564; and Cecil Angel, "In Detroit's Distressed Areas, the Neighbors Left, and Now Services Disappear," *Detroit Free Press*, May 20, 2012.

Chapter 3: Schools, Plus a Word about Crime

Page 79: Peter Karmanos Jr. anecdote: John Gallagher, "Karmanos' Detroit Odyssey Leads to Era of Hope," *Detroit Free Press*, Dec. 3, 1999.

Page 80: Detroit Public Schools' performance: Chastity Pratt Dawsey, "DPS Students Still Lagging in Reading, Math," *Detroit Free Press*, Dec. 8, 2011.

Page 81: Baylor-Woodson story: Based on author site visit and interviews Feb. 27, 2011; see also "What Our Students Deserve: Facing the Truth about Education in the Midwest States," published February 2012 by Education Trust-Midwest, accessed online at www.edtrust.org/sites/edtrust.org/files/publications/files/ETM%20Annual%20Report%202012%20What%20Our%20Students%20Deserve_0.pdf.

Page 81: Thomas Maridada story and quotes: Maridada keynote address, Rochester College Academic Symposium, April 19, 2011, available on YouTube at www.youtube.com/watch?v=K1OXdR6bZ6E.

Page 84: Tawanna Hudson quote: Karen Bouffard, "Inkster Sees Reawakening in Education: District Overcomes Financial Turmoil," *Detroit News, Sept. 19, 2006. Janice Lloyd quote: Melanie Scott, "Pontiac Sees New Promise," *Detroit Free Press*, July 13, 2009.

Page 85: Charlotte-Mecklenburg schools: See "Charlotte Mecklenburg Schools," accessed at www.cms.k12.nc.us/mediaroom/Documents/Charlotte-

Mecklenburg%20Schools.PDF; "Strategic Staffing," accessed at www.
cms.k12.nc.us/superintendent/White%20Papers/Strategic%20Staffing.pdf;
"Evaluation of the Strategic Staffing Initiative," accessed at http://media.
charlotteobserver.com/images/pdf/StrategicStaffEval.pdf.

Page 85: Amber Arellano: Author interview, Feb. 22, 2012, Royal Oak, MI.

Page 86: Dan Varner: Author interview, Feb. 16, 2012, Detroit.

Chapter 4: Economics

Page 93: Rick DeVos interview and ArtPrize story: Author interview, Jan. 27,
2012; see also "The Economic Impact of ArtPrize 2011," Anderson Economic
Group, accessed at www.andersoneconomicgroup.com/Publications/Detail/
tabid/125/articleType/ArticleView/articleId/8013/The-Economic-Impact-of-
ArtPrize-2011.aspx.

Page 96: Stratford story: "The Stratford Story," Stratford Festival, accessed at
www.stratfordfestival.ca/about/history.aspx?id=8217.

Page 97: Art

Serve Michigan report: "New Data Released by ArtServe Michigan Reveals
Significant Economic Impact by Michigan's Creative Sector," press release
and report from ArtServe Michigan, Jan. 23, 2012, accessed at www.
artservemichigan.org/20120123129/news/press-releases/new-data-released-
by-artserve-michigan-reveals-significant-economic-impact-by-michigans-
creative-sector/.

Page 98: Dan Kildee: Quote from Kildee land bank conference, June 6, 2011,
Detroit.

Page 99: TechTown companies: "Michigan Pre-seed Capital Fund Investment
Program Fuels Growth of TechTown Startups," Wayne State University press
release, March 20, 2011.

Page 100: Randal Charlton on entrepreneurship: Quoted in John Gallagher,
Reimagining Detroit: Opportunities for Redefining an American City (Detroit:
Wayne State University Press, 2010), 123.

Page 100: Bruce Katz: Author interview, Feb. 23, 2012, Detroit.

Page 101: Pittsburgh Duquesne Club anecdote: Xavier de Souza Briggs,
*Democracy as Problem Solving: Civic Capacity in Communities Across the
Globe* (Cambridge, MA: MIT Press, 2008), 166.

Page 101: Skip Simms and SPARK: John Gallagher, "State of Entrepreneurialism: Michigan Needs to do More Nurturing of Start-ups, Say People in the Know," *Detroit Free Press*, Oct. 28, 2011.

Page 102: Kauffman Entrepreneurial estimates: Kauffman Index of Entrepreneurial Activity, accessed at www.kauffman.org/research-and-policy/kauffman-index-of-entrepreneurial-activity.aspx. See also John Gallagher, "State Lags in Start-ups," *Detroit Free Press*, March 20, 2012.

Page 102: National Venture Capital Association: Data accessed at www.nvca.org/index.php?option=com_content&view=article&id=344&Itemid=103.

Page 102: Charles Ballard quote: John Gallagher, "State of Entrepreneurialism? Michigan Needs to Do More Nurturing of Start-ups, Say People in the Know," *Detroit Free Press*, Oct. 28, 2011.

Page 103: Dan Gilbert M@dison story: Based on author interviews and site visit Jan. 30, 2012; see also John Gallagher, "Giving Detroit a Digital Hub," *Detroit Free Press*, Jan. 31, 2012.

Page 106: Michigan losing 800,000 jobs in decade: Unemployment data for Detroit taken from Michigan Bureau of Labor Market Information, available at www.milmi.org/.

Page 106: Detroit's share of foreign-born citizens: See Brookings Institution, "Recent Immigration to Philadelphia: Regional Change in a Re-Emerging Gateway," 2008, accessed at www.brookings.edu/~/media/research/files/reports/2008/11/13%20immigration%20singer/1113_immigration_singer.pdf.

Page 107: Vinay Gupta: See Nathan Bomey, "Dual Entrepreneurs Reflect Next Stage of Ann Arbor's Startup Community," AnnArbor.com, Feb. 14, 2010, accessed at www.annarbor.com/business-review/dual-entrepreneurs-reflect-next-stage-of-ann-arbors-startup-community/.

Page 107: Snyder and Tobocman quotes: Katherine Yung, "Immigrant Start-ups Seen as Key to Reinventing Michigan," *Detroit Free Press*, Jan. 21, 2011.

Page 107: Global Detroit: See "Global Detroit Study" available at http://neweconomyinitiative.cfsem.org/resources/research-library/global-detroit-study.

Page 108: Blue Economy: John Gallagher, "Waters Have Potential to Bring in Jobs, Money, Experts Say," *Detroit Free Press*, June 5, 2011.

Page 109: Dave Egner: Gallagher, ibid.

Page 109: John Austin quote: Author interview, May 13, 2011, by phone.

Page 109: Cascade Engineering: John Gallagher, "Waters Have Potential to Bring in Jobs, Money, Experts Say," *Detroit Free Press*, June 5, 2011.

Page 110: UM Tech Transfer: Author interviews and site visit March 7, 2012. See also various articles at www.techtransfer.umich.edu/.

Page 112: Film credits: Katherine Yung, "Film Studio Struggles After State Says 'Cut!'" *Detroit Free Press*, March 18, 2012; and Katherine Yung and Julie Hinds, "Is That a Wrap on Movies?" *Detroit Free Press*, Feb. 18, 2011.

Page 113: Skip Simms quote: John Gallagher, "State of Entrepreneurialism? Michigan Needs to Do More nurturing of Start-ups, Say People in the Know," *Detroit Free Press*, Oct. 28, 2011.

Chapter 5: New Uses for Urban Land

Page 118: Almost 100,000 vacant lots: Detroit Residential Parcel Survey by Data Driven Detroit, accessed at http://datadrivendetroit.org/projects/detroit-residential-parcel-survey/. See also John Gallagher, "Many Are Gone, but More Remain," *Detroit Free Press*, Feb. 20, 2010.

Page 119: MSU study: Kathryn Colasanti and Michael Hamm, "Assessing the Local Food Supply Capacity of Detroit, Michigan," *Journal of Agriculture, Food Systems, and Community Development*, published online November 2010, accessed at www.agdevjournal.com/attachments/137_JAFSCD_Assessing_Food_Supply_Capacity_Detroit_Nov-2010.pdf.

Page 120: Joan Moss: Author interview, Feb. 20, 2012, Detroit.

Page 120: Side lots: Author interview with Dewar, Nov. 7, 2011; see also Margaret Dewar and Robert Linn, "Remaking Brightmoor," draft of book chapter made available to author by Prof. Dewar.

Page 121: Blots: Tobias Armborst, Daniel D'Oca, and Georgeen Theodore, "Improve Your Lot!" in *Cities Growing Smaller*, vol. 1 of *Urban Infill*, ed. Steve Rugare and Terry Schwarz (Kent, OH: Cleveland Urban Design Collaborative, 2008), 45–64.

Page 123: Philadelphia Green Vacant Lot restoration: See John Gallagher, "Filling the Vacancy" chapter in *Reimagining Detroit: Opportunities for Redefining an American City* (Detroit: Wayne State University Press, 2010). Also author interviews and site visits in 2009 and 2011.

Page 124: Susan Wachter paper: "The Determinants of Neighborhood
Transformations in Philadelphia—Identification and Analysis: The New
Kensington Pilot Study," The Wharton School, University of Pennsylvania,
2004, quoted in Gallagher, *Reimagining Detroit*.

Page 124: Dr. Charles C. Branas' paper on crime in vacant lots reclaimed by
Philadelphia Green: Charles Branas, et al., "A Difference-in-Differences
Analysis of Health, Safety, and Greening Vacant Urban Space," *American
Journal of Epidemiology*, published online Nov. 11, 2011, accessed
at http://aje.oxfordjournals.org/content/early/2011/11/11/aje.kwr273.
abstract?sid=a6761918-eda3-4390-8068-c4613cfddd61. See also Emily
Badger, "Greening Vacant Lots Linked to Reduced Gun Violence," *The
Atlantic* Cities, Nov. 2, 2011, accessed online at www.theatlanticcities.
com/neighborhoods/2011/11/greening-vacant-lots-linked-reduced-gun-
violence/526/.

Page 128: Riet Schumack: Site visit and author interviews, Detroit, Sept. 25,
2011.

Page 131: Spring Gardens story: Site visits and author interviews 2009 and 2010.

Page 136: Gary Wozniak story: Based on multiple author interviews and site
visits with Wozniak over the 2010–2012 period; see also John Gallagher,
"Growing Pains Hit Urban Farm Plans: Detroit Officials Slow to OK Projects on
Zoning Concerns," *Detroit Free Press*, Nov. 13, 2010.

Page 140: Hantz Farms story: Based on multiple author interviews and site
visits with John Hantz and Michael Score in the 2009–2012 period; see also
John Gallagher, "Finally Growing: Hantz Farms Begins Planting Saplings
in Detroit," *Detroit Free Press*, Nov. 19, 2011; and John Gallagher, "Farming
Struggles to Grow in the City: Detroit Officials Slow to Embrace Agricultural
Plans," *Detroit Free Press*, Aug. 8, 2011.

Page 141: Park Supermarket in Holland: Author interview. See also George
Webster, "Farm in the City Could Be Supermarket of the Future," CNN, Oct.
29, 2011, accessed at www.cnn.com/2011/10/29/world/europe/holland-park-
supermarket/index.html.

Page 144: Steve Vogel: Author interview, Sept. 23, 2011, Detroit. See also John
Gallagher, "Bloody Run's Bright Potential," *Detroit Free Press*, May 9, 2011.

Page 149: Mitch Cope: Site visit and author interview, Jan. 31, 2012. In June

2012, ArtPlace, a national coalition of foundations, banks, and federal agencies, awarded PowerHouse Productions a $250,000 grant to transform three vacant homes into spaces for art, theater, and recreation programming. See Mark Stryker, "ArtPlace Gives Budding Detroit Project Venerable DIA Grants Totaling More Than $500,000," *Detroit Free Press*, June 12, 2012.

Page 151: Heidelberg Project: Site visit and author interviews Sept. 25, 2011.

Page 153: Philadelphia Mural Arts: Site visit and author interviews with Jane Golden and Cesar Viveros, Oct. 1, 2012.

Page 157: Hunter Morrison: Site visit and author interview, Jan. 24, 2011.

Page 158: LEAP project: John Gallagher, "Group Has Detailed Plan to Improve Lower East-side Detroit Neighborhood," *Detroit Free Press*, Sept. 4, 2011, accessed at http://datadrivendetroit.org/web_ftp/News/Freep_090411.pdf.

Page 158: Maggie DeSantis quote: Author interview, July 29, 2011.

Page 160: Constance Bodurow: Author interview, Oct. 24, 2011, Detroit.

Chapter 6: Learning from Europe

Page 164: (Manchester and Leipzig sections) Based on author visits and interviews as part of the German Marshall Fund of the United States' Cities in Transition program conducted in December 2010. See also "Shrinking Cities" Working Papers accessed at www.gmfus.org/galleries/cdp-tcn/Cities_in_Transition_Stakeholder_Briefing_Materials__FINAL.pdf.

INDEX